Thanks for looking after Sam the Man ... I saw this book & thought of you both
Cheers Justine xo

PARTY CAKES
for Kiwi Kids

First published in 2009 by New Holland Publishers (NZ) Ltd
Auckland • Sydney • London • Cape Town

www.newhollandpublishers.co.nz

218 Lake Road, Northcote, Auckland 0627, New Zealand
Unit 1, 66 Gibbes Street, Chatswood, NSW 2067, Australia
86–88 Edgware Road, London W2 2EA, United Kingdom
80 McKenzie Street, Cape Town 8001, South Africa

Commissioning editor: Louise Armstrong
Project manager: Georgina McWhirter
Editor: Sarah Elworthy
Designer: Renee Greenland

National Library of New Zealand Cataloguing-in-Publication Data

Hislop, Annette.
Party cakes for Kiwi kids / written by Annette Hislop and Linda Ross ;
photography by Nicola Topping.
Includes index.
ISBN 978-1-86966-248-6
1. Cake decorating. 2. Birthday cakes.
I. Ross, Linda, 1963- II. Topping, Nicola. III. Title.
641.8653—dc 22

1 3 5 7 9 10 8 6 4 2

Colour reproduction by Image Centre Ltd
Printed by Times Offset (M) Sdn Bhd, Malaysia, on paper sourced from sustainable forests.

PARTY CAKES for Kiwi Kids

Annette Hislop & Linda Ross

Photography by Nicola Topping

NEW HOLLAND

HAPPY BIRTHDAY

JACKSON
11

CONTENTS

INTRODUCTION

With five children between us, we have hosted and attended many birthday parties. Along the way we have seen our fair share of cakes and, like most parents, have been amazed by some of the creations we have encountered.

Many of us want to make a birthday cake for our kids that is memorable, but have different abilities and time constraints. Living in New Zealand we are lucky to have long hot summers and many sporting and outdoor-adventure pursuits to indulge in alongside our kids. With these things in mind, we put our heads together to create a book featuring party cakes with a distinct Kiwi flavour – as well as some of the classics – which would appeal to cooks of all abilities.

The fastest and most popular way of decorating a cake is to use buttercream icing and lollies. These cakes are always a hit – after all, what child can resist the lure of all that sugar!

Sometimes, however, the party theme calls for something a little more special, and for these cakes we found that using sugarpaste icing not only resulted in a cleaner, more professional finish, but allowed us to make figures and accessories that would be almost impossible to create by any other means. The more you work with sugarpaste, the quicker and better you become at using it, and we have also included a list of hints and tips for those of you using sugarpaste for the first time to help you become more confident.

Please note, we have included suggestions for breaking up the work involved into two days for some of the more involved cakes so that you are never asked to do too much work on the day of the party.

You will find that as a general rule we have recommended our one-star cakes be made the day of the party as they are relatively easy to prepare while our three-star cakes are best completed the day before the party as they are more time-consuming and fiddly. The work involved in creating two-star cakes we have generally advised splitting across two days.

Alternatively, any cake that uses only *sugarpaste icing* could be completed a day or two before it is needed, if you do not wish to do any work on the day of the party. Simply store the finished cake loosely wrapped in a tea towel in a warm, dry place until required. On the other hand, cakes that use *buttercream icing* are best iced on the day or the icing may run or break down.

Provided you stick to our advice we are sure you'll have success. Adapt a cake to suit your child's interests and your party theme and don't worry if it is not perfect. Chances are everyone else will think it is!

We hope you enjoy making these cakes as much as we did.

Annette Hislop and Linda Ross

EQUIPMENT

Below you will find a list of kitchen tools that are useful for cake making and decorating and will help you achieve a professional-looking result.

1. **BAKING PAPER**

   Baking paper is a must in the kitchen. Not only is it invaluable for lining cake tins, it is also perfect for laying sugarpaste figures and accessories on to dry, as they won't stick. Since baking paper is translucent, it is also ideal for tracing templates (see Using templates, page 13). Sugarpaste can also be rolled directly onto baking paper when making cake decorations.

2. **SCALES**

   A good set of scales takes the guesswork out of measuring cake and icing ingredients and ensures accuracy. Digital scales are the most accurate and will give you the best results.

3. **CAKE TINS**

   It is worth building up a set of good-quality tins, as these will last a lifetime. Wash and dry them thoroughly after each use. Choose heavier tins as these won't buckle or become misshapen. It is a good idea to line them to ensure the cake comes out cleanly.

   Square adjustable cake tins come in two halves which can slide apart to create a larger rectangular shape. These are very handy to have as they can take the place of a cupboard full of various-sized tins.

   Cakes can also be baked in metal bowls, fruit tins and terracotta pots, but make sure they are well lined with baking paper.

4. **SCISSORS**

   Needed for cutting templates.

5. **RULER**

   Useful for measuring when cutting sugarpaste or cake or making a template.

6. **CUTTERS**

   Biscuit or cookie cutters are invaluable for decorating as they cut uniform shapes and letters out of sugarpaste. Metal cutters are the best to use as they produce a nice clean edge.

Cookie cutters are readily available from cake decorating suppliers and kitchenware stores, often in sets. If you don't want all the cutters in a set, team up with a friend, buy one or two different sets each and share them.

7. ICING NOZZLES

Plain round icing nozzles come in handy when a tiny circle is needed, for example in creating the spots on the Kiwi party cake (see page 39). They are also the perfect size for pressing smiles into the faces of sugarpaste figures.

8. FOOD COLOURING GELS OR PASTES

Food colouring gels or pastes give the best results when colouring icing. Although they can be expensive, they will last for years and are worth investing in. These are available from specialist cake decorating suppliers and some kitchenware stores.

9. KNIVES

Sharp, flat-bladed knives are best for cutting sugarpaste.

10. PASTRY BRUSH

A pastry brush is useful for brushing sieved and thinned jam onto cakes before covering with sugarpaste to ensure the icing sticks and for removing excess icing sugar from sugarpaste.

11. ROLLING PIN

Choose a perfectly smooth rolling pin, especially when working with sugarpaste as any marks will show up.

12. SKEWERS AND TOOTHPICKS

Thick skewers are perfect to use when you need to make a large hole, for instance when attaching arms to bodies, while thin bamboo skewers or toothpicks can be helpful when a cake needs support, such as the Lamington castle (see page 14).

13. SUGAR ART PENS

Sugar art pens contain edible ink and are used to write on sugarpaste. These are available from specialist cake decorating suppliers. Alternatively, you can use diluted food colouring gel and paint onto sugarpaste using a fine paintbrush.

14. CAKE DECORATING WIRE

Cake decorating wire is available from specialist cake decorating suppliers and some kitchenware stores. Use this when you want to suspend objects above a cake, for instance, the flying stars and boulders on the Volcano cake (see page 18).

15. DRIED SPAGHETTI

Pieces of dried spaghetti are useful for attaching pieces of sugarpaste together. They are sturdy enough to hold the parts firmly and are edible, unlike toothpicks.

WORKING WITH SUGARPASTE

We have used ready-made sugarpaste icing to cover a number of the cakes in this book. Sometimes called fondant, white icing or ready-to-roll icing, sugarpaste comes in 500 g or 750 g packets and is readily available in the baking section of most supermarkets and from specialist cake decorating suppliers.

We have found the Bakels Pettinice white icing (which comes in a 750 g pack) to be a particularly good and malleable sugarpaste but there are other brands available if you can't find it.

Sugarpaste is very easy to use, but for those of you unfamiliar with it, we have included some of the tips and tricks we have learnt along the way.

COLOURING SUGARPASTE

Lightly dust your work surface with icing sugar, and knead the sugarpaste well to make it soft and pliable before using.

Use only good-quality food colouring gels, available from cake decorating suppliers, when colouring sugarpaste. Liquid food colourings make the icing too wet and don't give such an intense colour.

Add a small amount of food colouring gel using the tip of a small knife or a toothpick to the sugarpaste and knead in.

Continue to add a little more at a time to deepen the hue until you achieve the desired colour. The colours are very concentrated and will intensify over time. This is important to keep in mind when making dark colours, especially red and black.

When colouring a large quantity of icing, work the gel into a small piece of the sugarpaste first, then knead this into the remaining larger piece.

Sugarpaste can be coloured up to a few days in advance. Keep sugarpaste well wrapped in plastic food wrap whenever you are not using it as it dries out very quickly. Don't store it in the fridge, and don't get it wet.

COVERING A CAKE WITH SUGARPASTE

Before rolling out the sugarpaste, ensure your work surface is completely clean and smooth. Make sure there are no crumbs as they are sugarpaste's number one enemy! Ensure too, that your rolling pin has no dents or grooves as these will show up on the icing.

Dust the work surface very lightly with icing sugar, but try not to use too much as it will stick to the sugarpaste and can be tricky to remove. If you do get a build-up, brush it away using a pastry brush.

Roll out the icing to the required size, and remember that when covering a cake, the sugarpaste needs to be at least 4 mm thick to produce a good smooth finish.

Brush the cake with sieved apricot jam that has been thinned with a little hot water. This will help the sugarpaste stick to the cake.

Roll the sugarpaste loosely around a rolling pin to transfer it over the cake, then smooth down the icing with the heel of your hand, rubbing in circular motions to help even it out.

You can rub any small tears or nicks firmly with your fingers to seal the edges together.

MAKING SUGARPASTE DECORATIONS AND FIGURES

Sugarpaste is excellent for making decorations such as people, animals or shapes. It just needs to be coloured, then shaped and left to harden before using on your cake. Most decorations can be made up to a few days in advance.

One of the most time-consuming parts of making figures is colouring the sugarpaste, especially when you have a few colours to make. However remember that this can be done up to a few days in advance. Simply wrap the coloured sugarpaste well in plastic food wrap to prevent it drying out until needed.

Once you have shaped your decorations, lay the pieces out to harden on baking paper. Cover them loosely (they need to be able to breathe) and leave in a warm, dry place – a cardboard box in a hot water cupboard is perfect.

If you live in a humid area, you may find that the sugarpaste takes longer to harden.

TIPS FOR MODELLING FIGURES:

- Pressing on smiles can be tricky. We found that the end of a small plain icing nozzle was perfect for this job (see below), but you can just as easily use the end of a felt pen lid or something of a similar size and shape.

- To attach sugarpaste limbs and features such as arms, legs, necks, noses and ears, it is best to poke a hole with a thick skewer in the body where the part will be attached (see below), then mould the features with tapered ends into the hole.

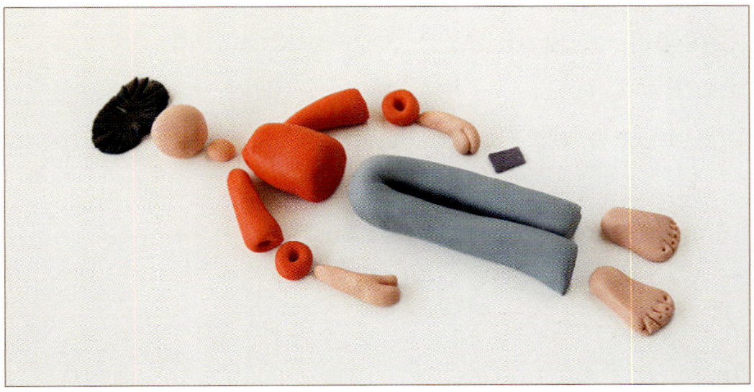

- The easiest way to make trousers or legs is to roll one long piece of sugarpaste and fold it in half, so that you have a little bottom for the torso to sit on (see above). Trim the hems of the trousers with scissors or a sharp knife to tidy them up.

BASIC RECIPES

On the following two pages we have provided recipes for a chocolate cake and a Madeira cake. These are both good, fairly dense cakes suitable for cutting into shapes.

You can use store-bought cakes or make one from a packet mix but these are often too soft and crumbly, making them difficult to sculpt. However, they are fine for cakes that require little or no cutting.

Be aware that packet cake mixtures vary in quality – some are quite good, others not so good – so it pays to try a few to find one that you like.

MADEIRA CAKE

200 g butter
200 g caster sugar
4 eggs
200 g plain flour
1 teaspoon baking powder
1 tablespoon milk

Preheat the oven to 180°C.

Line a 23 cm round cake tin with baking paper.

Soften the butter, then beat the butter with the sugar until the mixture is light and fluffy.

Beat in the eggs one at a time. If the mixture looks like it is curdling, beat in 1 tablespoon of the measured flour to stabilise it.

Sift together the flour and baking powder, fold this into the creamed mixture and stir in the milk.

Spoon the mixture into the prepared tin and bake for about 45 minutes or until a skewer comes out clean. Transfer to a wire rack to cool.

CHOCOLATE CAKE

125 g butter
125 g dark chocolate
1 cup sugar
1 teaspoon vanilla essence
3 eggs
1 cup buttermilk or plain unsweetened yoghurt
1¼ cups plain flour
¼ cup cocoa
1½ teaspoons baking powder
½ teaspoon baking soda
½ teaspoon salt

Preheat the oven to 180°C.

Line a 23 cm round cake tin with baking paper.

Place the butter and chocolate into a small metal or glass bowl and set over a small saucepan of barely simmering water. When the chocolate begins to melt, stir to combine it with the butter.

When the mixture is smooth, remove from the heat, add the sugar and vanilla essence and mix well.

Lightly beat the eggs and add them to the mixture along with the buttermilk or yoghurt. Stir well and transfer to a larger bowl.

Sift together the flour, cocoa, baking powder, baking soda and salt, then add this to the chocolate mixture. Mix well.

Spoon the mixture into the prepared tin and bake for about 50 minutes or until a skewer comes out clean. Transfer to a wire rack to cool.

CHOCOLATE BUTTERCREAM ICING

100 g butter, softened
1¾ cups icing sugar
¼ cup cocoa powder
a little hot water

Beat the butter in a small bowl with an electric mixer until it turns almost white.

Sift together the icing sugar and cocoa powder, then mix this into the butter along with a little hot water. Beat until you have a smooth, light-textured icing.

BUTTERCREAM ICING

100 g butter, softened
2 cups icing sugar
a little hot water

Beat the butter in a small bowl with an electric mixer until it turns almost white.

Gradually sift in the icing sugar, along with a little hot water, and beat until you have a fluffy, light-textured icing.

USING A CRUMB COAT

When you cut a cake to shape it you invariably create plenty of crumbs. To prevent these getting into your buttercream icing and ruining the finish, you may like to ice the cake with a 'crumb coat' first.

This is simply a thin layer of buttercream icing spread over the cake which will collect and hold all the crumbs in place. Leave the icing to dry for a few minutes before covering with your main and final buttercream coating.

USING TEMPLATES

Templates for some of our cake shapes and decorative figures are provided in the back of the book. To make these motifs, cover the template with a sheet of baking paper. Knead the sugarpaste until it is soft and pliable, then place an appropriately sized ball of it in the centre of the template shape (visible through the baking paper). Use your fingers to mould the sugarpaste to fill in the outline. Place on the cake immediately or store in plastic food wrap until needed.

To cut the cakes that use a template, trace the template onto baking paper and cut out. Place this pattern on the cake and cut around the outline with a serrated knife.

RATING

Next to each cake's name is a degree-of-difficulty rating:

★ These are the quickest and easiest cakes to prepare and can be made the day of the party.

★★ These make use of sugarpaste and/or the cutting and shaping of the cake. We have usually suggested the work be split across two days.

★★★ These cakes are the most time-consuming and involve modelling sugarpaste. They can be made the day before the party.

LAMINGTON CASTLE

Children everywhere dream of being king or queen of their own castle. Making their dream come true is easy using store-bought lamingtons and ice cream cones. Hide some lollies under the cones for an extra treat.

WHAT YOU'LL NEED

CAKE

200 g sugarpaste icing
16 chocolate lamingtons

DECORATIONS

6 ice cream cones
150 g chocolate
1 cup icing sugar
brown food colouring gel
4 thin chocolate sticks

SPECIAL EQUIPMENT

long skewers
paper (see note on page 17)
glue stick or sticky tape

ON THE DAY OF THE PARTY

COATING THE ICE CREAM CONES

1. Start by covering the ice cream cones in chocolate. Melt the chocolate either in a bowl over a saucepan of gently simmering water or by microwaving it in 30-second bursts until the chocolate begins to melt. Stir until smooth.

2. Poke a long wooden skewer down through the top of the first cone. Hold this over the bowl of melted chocolate and use a spoon to coat the cone with chocolate. Suspend over a container to dry.

3. Repeat with the remaining cones (it is a good idea to do an extra cone in case one comes to grief – this can always be eaten if you don't need it!).

4. Once the chocolate on the cones is set, carefully remove the skewers and set aside.

MAKING THE DOORS AND WINDOWS

1. Take 100 g of the sugarpaste and colour it brown (see Colouring sugarpaste, page 10). Wrap well in plastic food wrap and set aside.

2. Lightly dust your work surface with icing sugar and roll the 100 g of white sugarpaste out to about 2 mm.

3. Cut out two square windows (2 cm x 2 cm), and three rectangle windows (2 cm x 4 cm) and one rectangle door (2 cm x 6 cm). Cut the top of the door into a triangular peak.

4. Roll the brown sugarpaste out to 2 mm thickness.

5. Lay the windows and door on top of the brown sugarpaste. Use a sharp knife to cut around them so that there is a 2 mm frame of brown showing around the edges of the doors and windows.

6. Add a brown sugarpaste door handle to the door. Set the windows and doors aside.

7. Cut five long, thin triangular flags out of paper, and using a glue stick or sticky tape, attach each one to the blunt end of five skewers.

ASSEMBLING THE CAKE

1. Place the icing sugar into a small bowl and mix with enough hot water to make the consistency of pouring cream. You will use this mixture as a glue to hold the castle together.

2. To make the tallest tower, stack four lamingtons on top of each other, spreading a little icing sugar 'glue' mixture between each to help stick them together. Carefully position this onto a flat serving tray.

3. Make two medium-sized towers using three lamingtons for each, gluing together with the icing sugar mixture.

4. Make three short towers using two lamingtons for each, gluing together with the icing sugar mixture.

5. Arrange the two middle-sized lamington towers on either side of the tallest tower.

6. Place the three shorter towers in the front.

7. Using the icing sugar glue, position one of the two square windows onto each middle-sized tower, and one rectangle window onto the tallest tower and the remaining two rectangle windows onto the two short towers at the front sides.

8. Glue the door to the centre short tower.

9. Place a chocolate-coated cone on top of each tower, except the centre door tower.

10. Run a flagged skewer down through the cone and the lamingtons to secure them.

11. Arrange the chocolate sticks to make a drawbridge.

NOTE:

- *Although they may appear nice and square in the packet, lamingtons are often uneven and can present a challenge when stacking – it may pay to have some extra on hand just in case.*

- *Make the flags any colour you like – you could write your child's age or initials on them too.*

- *This cake does not travel well, so if possible assemble it at the table or at least close by.*

- *A large party can be catered for by adding more lamingtons with windows and towers.*

- *If you want a smaller cake try making a lamington cottage (see below). Using the steps in the Lamington Castle recipe as a guide make a smaller structure with shorter towers and no chocolate-coated ice cream cones. Shape the top of the three back towers into triangular peaks and top each with a sugarpaste roof. Make flowers and swirls as described in the Flowerpot cake (see page 54) and add mini marshmallows to complete the effect.*

VOLCANO CAKE

This large and dramatic cake makes a sensational centrepiece. Made from rice bubbles and chocolate, it requires no cooking and has a truly rugged volcanic look. As it is hollow you can hide lollies under it for an extra surprise.

WHAT YOU'LL NEED

CAKE

100 g white sugarpaste icing
5 cups rice bubbles
500 g cooking chocolate

DECORATIONS

50 g butter
2½ cups icing sugar
red food colouring gel
orange or yellow food colouring gel
Cadbury Jaffas
chocolate raisins
orange Nestlé Wonka Nerds lollies, or similar

SPECIAL EQUIPMENT

3 cm star cutter
1.8 litre rounded bowl
cake decorating wire

THE DAY BEFORE THE PARTY

MAKING THE STARS AND THE RICE BUBBLE CAKE

1. Make the flying stars by rolling out the white sugarpaste to a thickness of 5 mm on a work surface very lightly dusted with icing sugar.

2. Cut out five or six stars and lay on a sheet of baking paper in a warm, dry place to harden.

3. Make the 'cake' by covering the outside of a 1.8 litre-capacity round bowl with plastic food wrap. Place this upside down on a large plate.

4. Place the rice bubbles into a large bowl and set aside.

5. Melt chocolate in a bowl over a saucepan of barely simmering water or heat in 30-second bursts in the microwave. Once the chocolate is beginning to melt, take off the element or from the microwave and stir until smooth.

6. Pour the chocolate over the rice bubbles and mix until well coated.

7. Using two dessertspoons, pile the mixture over the plastic food wrap-covered bowl. It will slide around a bit at first but as the chocolate begins to firm up, it will start to stick well.

8. Use the back of a spoon to form a crater in the top.

9. As the mixture cools, use your hands to mould it into shape around the bowl.

10. Cover with a fly net food tent and set aside in a cool place to harden.

ON THE DAY OF THE PARTY

1. Remove the basin from the volcano by pouring a little boiling water down the sides and into the bowl and swirling it around a bit. This should soften the chocolate sufficiently for the bowl to pop out, but don't leave the water in for too long or you will melt the chocolate and the volcano may collapse.

2. Place on a large flat serving plate or tray.

3. Melt the butter and add the icing sugar and enough warm water to make it the consistency of pouring cream. Divide this mixture in half and colour half of it red and the other half orange.

4. Pour the red icing carefully over the top and down the sides of the volcano so that it resembles flowing lava. Leave to cool and harden.

5. You will need to soften the orange icing before pouring it. Give it a few short bursts in the microwave until it is softened enough, then pour over the red icing.

6. While the icing is still soft, stud in a few Jaffas, Nerds and chocolate raisins.

7. Carefully poke the wire into the sides of the sugarpaste stars and also a few chocolate-coated raisins.

8. Bend the wire around a jar so that you get a nice even curve and then poke the ends into the top of the volcano so that the rocks and stars appear to fly out of the crater.

KIWI IN THE WILD

★ ★ ★

Kiwi are elusive birds, so give everyone a chance to see them in this cute kiwi cake with its burrow and hidden egg tucked around the back. The templates on page 93 make forming the kiwi and trees easy.

WHAT YOU'LL NEED

CAKE

900 g sugarpaste icing
1 quantity chocolate cake mixture (see Basic recipes, page 12)

DECORATIONS

moss green food colouring gel
brown food colouring gel
golden yellow food colouring gel
sieved apricot jam, thinned with a little hot water

SPECIAL EQUIPMENT

20 cm (1.5 litre) pudding bowl
baking paper
pastry brush
toothpick

THE DAY BEFORE THE PARTY

MAKING THE CAKE

1. Bake the cake in the pudding bowl lined with baking paper. Once cooked, set upside down on a serving plate to cool.

COLOURING THE SUGARPASTE

1. Set aside 50 g of white sugarpaste to make the egg and eyes for the kiwi.

2. Take 400 g of sugarpaste and knead in enough green food colouring gel to produce a pale green for covering the cake.

3. For the foliage, colour 100 g of sugarpaste a mid green and 100 g of sugarpaste a dark green by adding varying amounts of green food colouring gel.

4. Using the same method, colour 100 g of sugarpaste pale brown for the kiwi and 100 g a darker brown for the tree trunks.

5. Colour 50 g of sugarpaste golden yellow for the beaks and feet. Wrap all seven balls of icing in plastic food wrap and set aside.

ICING THE CAKE

1. At the cake base, carve out a hollow for the burrow about 4 cm high. This is where the egg will be hidden.

2. Brush the cake with the sieved and thinned apricot jam.

3. Lightly dust your work surface with icing sugar and roll the pale green sugarpaste into a circle that will just fit over the cake.

4. Carefully roll it around a rolling pin and transfer it to the cake. Smooth down carefully, trim off any excess and tuck the edges under neatly.

5. Lay a sheet of baking paper over the template provided on page 93 (see Using templates, page 13), and form two large and one small kiwi bodies out of the pale brown sugarpaste.

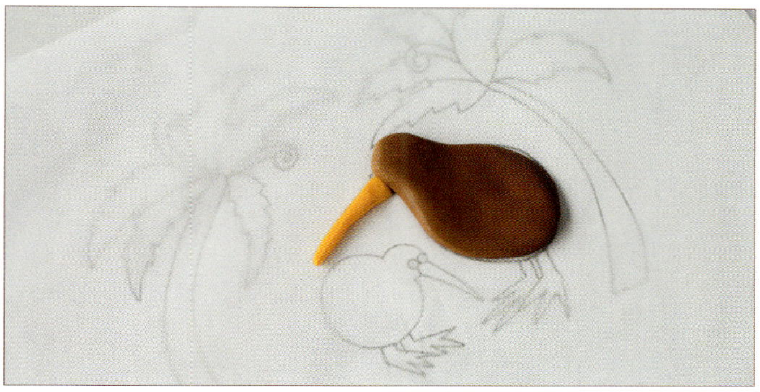

6. Use the guide to shape the beaks and feet separately out of the golden yellow sugarpaste. Cut out the toes.

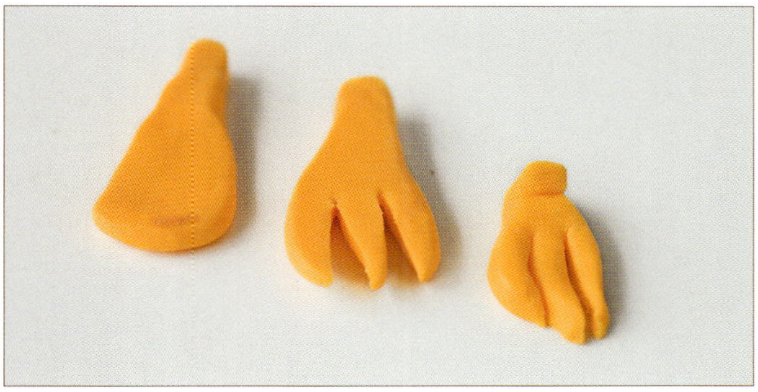

7. Position the kiwi bodies and feet onto the side of the cake, then place the ends of the beaks slightly under each of the heads.

8. Roll tiny balls of white for the eyes. Position the eyes on the kiwi and gently indent a pupil into each eye with a toothpick.

9. Using the darker brown sugarpaste, form three tree trunks and press these onto the side of the cake.

10. Use the templates to shape foliage out of the mid and dark green sugarpaste. Cut leaves using a small sharp knife. Transfer onto the tree trunks (see note below).

11. Shape an egg from the white sugarpaste and pop it into the burrow.

12. Using any leftover green sugarpaste, make foliage for the forest floor. Use the side of a spoon to press securely onto the cake. You can tidy up the bottom of the cake by pressing a thin roll of green icing around the edge.

13. Use up any remaining brown sugarpaste to make a few rocks to position around the base of the cake.

14. Store overnight in a warm, dry place, covered loosely with a tea towel.

NOTE: Sugarpaste items should stick to the cake but if you are concerned that they aren't secure, use a little brush and a tiny drop of water to glue them. If you use too much water the sugarpaste will dissolve, so be very careful.

PACIFICA MERMAID ★★★

This beautiful mermaid swimming in a marbled ocean looks complicated, but shaping her is not difficult if you follow the instructions and use the template at the back of the book. We suggest you complete this cake, or at least the sugarpaste decorations, the day before your event.

WHAT YOU'LL NEED

CAKE

950 g sugarpaste icing
23 cm round cake (see Basic recipes, page 12)
sieved apricot jam, thinned with a little hot water

DECORATIONS

royal blue food colouring gel
black food colouring gel
skin-toned food colouring gel
mint green food colouring gel
brown food colouring gel
silver cachous
edible silver lustre

SPECIAL EQUIPMENT

17 cm plate
pastry brush
toothpick
small plain round icing nozzle

THE DAY BEFORE THE PARTY

MAKING THE CAKE

1. Bake the cake and set aside to cool.

COLOURING THE SUGARPASTE

1. To make the marbled background, take 400 g of white sugarpaste and colour it royal blue, remembering that the colour will intensify over time (see Colouring sugarpaste, page 10). Divide this blue sugarpaste in half. Knead 300 g of white sugarpaste into half the blue sugarpaste to make a pale blue.

2. Roll the royal and light blue sugarpastes into long rolls, then twist together.

3. Form into two rolls again and twist together once more. Repeat this process a few more times to get a marbled effect, then roll into a ball.

4. Colour 20 g of sugarpaste pale grey (using a little black food colouring gel) and 50 g of sugarpaste skin tone.

5. For the tail, colour 50 g of sugarpaste a blue-green, using a suitable mixture of the mint green and royal blue food colouring gels.

6. Take three 30 g pieces of sugarpaste and colour one dark green, one pale green and one brown.

7. Set aside the remaining white sugarpaste.

8. Wrap all the sugarpaste in plastic food wrap as you work to prevent it drying out until ready to use.

ICING THE CAKE

1. Place the cake upside down on a serving plate or tray, so that you have a nice flat top for icing, and brush with the sieved and thinned apricot jam.

2. Lightly dust your work surface with icing sugar, then take the blue marbled icing and knead it slightly. Roll it into a circle large enough to just cover the cake.

3. Lay the icing carefully over the top of the cake, smooth down and cut off any excess.

4. Take a 17 cm plate and press this onto the top of the cake to indent a circle in the icing. You will use this as a guide when positioning the fish and cachous later.

MAKING THE MERMAID MOTIF

1. To make the mermaid, lay a sheet of baking paper over the template provided on page 92 (see Using templates, page 13).

2. Shape the mermaid's head and the neck using the skin-toned sugarpaste.

3. Make a tiny nose and ears and press on. Using a toothpick, poke holes where the ears and nose are to go and mould the sugarpaste ears and nose into these holes to secure. Use cachous for the earrings.

4. Shape one long arm from skin-toned sugarpaste, forming a hand at each end. Curl this around to sit on the template. Form the torso and lay over the arm.

5. Poke in eyes and the belly button using a toothpick and use the end of the small plain round icing nozzle to form a smile. Set the body parts aside.

6. Form the tail out of the blue-green icing, making the tail fins as a separate piece.

7. Looking at the iced cake, decide which part of the marbling looks the best and position the mermaid so that this part is not covered.

8. Place the mermaid on top of the cake about 2 cm inside the indented circle. Firstly position the arm pieces and then lay the torso over the top, pressing together gently. Tuck the neck under the torso slightly and then place on her head. Finally lay on her tail and fins, tucking the tail under the torso.

9. Use the small end of a plain round icing nozzle to press scales onto her tail. Press fin details into the tail using the edge of a teaspoon.

10. To make the scallop-shell bikini top, take two tiny pieces of white sugarpaste and roll them into two balls. Flatten out one side of each ball and pinch the other side slightly. Mark a scallop pattern using a sharp knife. Press the bikini onto the mermaid's chest and poke a silver cachou between the shells.

11. Make the hair by taking balls of brown sugarpaste and rolling them into strands in the palm of your hand. Place one end slightly under the head – these need to be long, random and flowing.

12. Make the fish bodies using the pale green sugarpaste, and the fins and tail from the dark green. Use the plain round icing nozzle to press scales onto the fish, and a toothpick to mark out the eyes.

13. If you like, use up any leftover green sugarpaste to make seaweed and press it onto the edges of the cake using the edge of a teaspoon. Otherwise leave the edges plain.

14. Roll out the grey sugarpaste to a thickness of 3–4 mm and cut out a few starfish using the template as a guide or a small star cutter.

15. Roll any remaining grey sugarpaste into small rocks and place around the base of the cake.

16. Position the fish, starfish and cachous around the mermaid, using the indented circle as a guide.

17. Finally, brush a little edible silver lustre (available at specialist cake decoration suppliers) onto the mermaid to make her shimmer.

18. Store overnight in a warm, dry place, covered loosely with a tea towel.

SUNDAY DRIVE

Discount stores are wonderful places to find small cars suitable for this cake.

WHAT YOU'LL NEED

CAKE

2 quantities Madeira cake mixture (see Basic recipes, page 12)
2½ quantities buttercream icing (see Basic recipes, page 13)

DECORATIONS

mint green food colouring gel
1 cup desiccated coconut
30 g chocolate hail
12 thin chocolate sticks
Nestlé Pixie Caramel Balls
Nestlé Wonka Nerds lollies
chocolate-coated raisins or peanuts
4–5 mini muffins of your choice
assorted green and yellow lollies
Nestlé Kit Kat 4 finger bar
spearmint leaves

SPECIAL EQUIPMENT

24 cm x 36 cm sponge-roll tin
baking paper
toothpicks
3 or more small toy cars

ON THE DAY OF THE PARTY

1. Bake the cake in the sponge-roll tin lined with baking paper that rises above the rim of the tin to contain any overflow.

2. When the cake has cooled completely place upside down on a large flat serving plate.

3. Make the buttercream icing and colour it mint green.

4. Place the coconut in a small plastic bag and add a dot of mint green food colouring gel. Knead together well.

5. Cover the sides and top of the cake with the green buttercream icing, saving some for covering the muffin trees.

6. Sprinkle the coloured coconut over the cake to form the grass.

7. Shake over the chocolate hail to form a winding road and halve the chocolate sticks and arrange as a roadside fence. Decorate the roadside with Pixie Caramel balls, chocolate-coated raisins or peanuts, and Nerds lollies.

8. To make the trees, cover the muffins with the reserved green icing and decorate with the green and yellow lollies. Press a Kit Kat finger into the base of each mini muffin and arrange on the cake.

9. Gently press toothpicks into the base of spearmint leaves and arrange as bushes. Finally, place the cars on the road, or substitute for plastic farm animals for a pastoral look.

TECHNO JUNKIE

This is a great cake for teenage children who are fanatical about computer games. Ideally, you should make this cake the day before as it is quite fiddly. Finish off the figure and accessories on the day if need be.

WHAT YOU'LL NEED

CAKE

½ quantity cake mixture (see Basic recipes, page 12) for the chair and footstool
23 cm round cake (see Basic recipes, page 12)
sieved apricot jam, thinned with a little hot water
about 1.5 kg sugarpaste

DECORATIONS

black food colouring gel
orange food colouring gel
Capri blue food colouring gel
skin-toned food colouring gel

SPECIAL EQUIPMENT

800 g tin can, well washed and label removed
baking paper
mini-muffin tray
pastry brush
large skewer
small plain round icing nozzle
dried spaghetti

THE DAY BEFORE THE PARTY

Colouring the sugarpaste can be done up to a few days in advance.

1. Take 400 g of sugarpaste and add a little black food colouring gel. Knead until you have a pale grey colour (see Colouring sugarpaste, page 10).

2. Colour 250 g of sugarpaste orange.

3. Colour 50 g Capri blue.

4. Colour a marble-sized piece of sugarpaste black for the hair.

5. Colour 30 g of sugarpaste skin tone.

6. Wrap all the pieces well in plastic food wrap and set aside.

MAKING THE CAKES

1. Bake the round cake.

2. To make the chair cake, line the tin can with two layers of baking paper. You will need a mini muffin for the footstool so divide the ½ quantity cake mixture between the tin can and one hole of a single lined mini-muffin tray.

Techno Freak

3. Cook the small cakes until a skewer pushed into the middle comes out clean. This will take around 20–30 minutes. Allow them to cool thoroughly before removing from the tins.

4. To shape the chair, cut a thin slice from one side of the tin can cake so that it has a flat side. Discard this piece, then cut a 2 cm thick slice for the chair back.

5. To make the seat of the chair, cut a third off the top of the remaining part of the tin can cake and carve out the seat and arms. Remember to make it big enough for the figure to sit on.

ICING THE CAKES

1. Brush the large round cake, the pieces of the chair and the mini muffin with apricot jam.

2. Very lightly dust your work surface with icing sugar, and roll out 700 g of white sugarpaste to a thickness of 4–5 mm so that it will completely cover the large cake.

3. Roll loosely around a rolling pin and carefully transfer it over the cake. Smooth down the sides and trim.

4. It is easiest to cover the chair in two parts. Roll out 150 g of grey sugarpaste and cover the back piece of the chair completely, then roll out another 150 g and cover the seat and arms, taking great care when moulding the sugarpaste around the arms to ensure it doesn't tear. Use a pair of scissors to trim it neatly.

5. Stick the two parts of the chair together by brushing it with sugar glue. Make this by mixing a little water into a knob of sugarpaste to create a thick slurry.

6. Roll out the remaining 50 g of grey sugarpaste to cover the mini muffin for the footstool.

7. For the rug, roll out 200 g of orange sugarpaste, and trim into a 20 cm square. Use a small sharp knife to cut a 1 cm fringe along two opposite edges.

8. Lay the rug on top of the large cake and position the chair and footstool towards the back of it.

MAKING THE FIGURE

1. Roll the blue sugarpaste into a tube 18 cm long, flaring it slightly for the ends of the jeans. Trim the ends with a sharp knife or scissors. Fold in half and place on the chair with one leg of the jeans resting on top of the footstool.

2. Use a tiny square of grey to make a patch for the knee of the jeans.

3. Take 40 g of the orange sugarpaste and shape two-thirds of it into a rectangle for the shirt body.

4. Shape the remaining piece into a 10 cm x 1 cm roll for the sleeves and cut in half. Form into two elongated carrot shapes and two donut-shaped pieces for the shirt cuffs.

5. Use the skewer to make holes in the shoulder of the shirt in which to position the carrot-shaped sleeves. Poke the sleeves in firmly and press the cuffs onto the bottom of the sleeves.

6. Position the t-shirt on top of the legs.

7. Take half the skin-toned sugarpaste and shape a head and a neck piece.

8. Use the skewer to poke a hole at the neck of the t-shirt. Place a short stick of spaghetti into this neck hole and press the neck piece over it. Position the head on top.

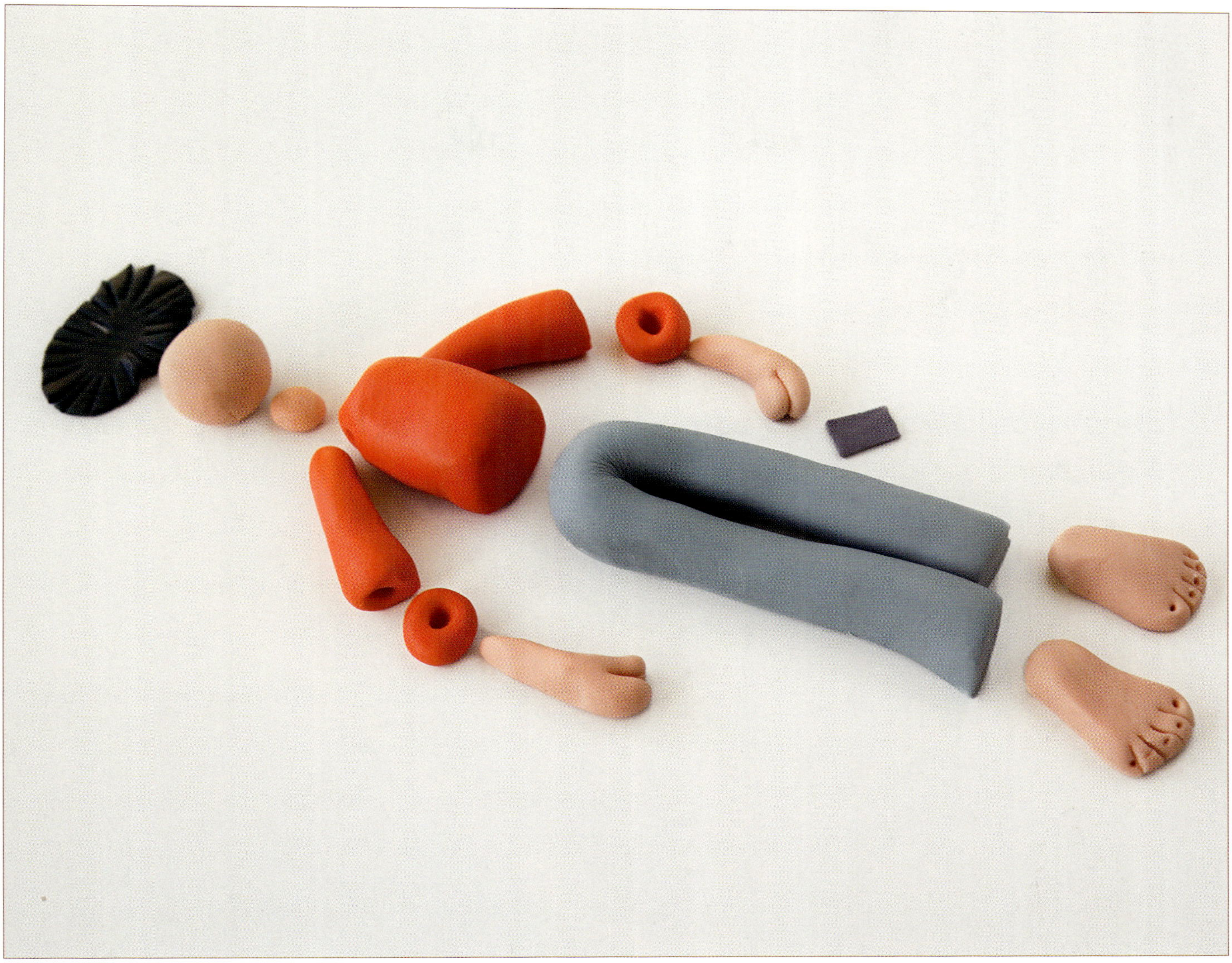

9. Poke in eyes with the skewer and a smile with the end of a plain round icing nozzle.

10. Take a tiny piece of skin tone and roll into a ball for the nose, shaping one side to a point.

11. Poke a hole in the centre of the face and mould the pointy end of the nose into it.

12. Roll two tiny ears and attach as you did for the nose.

13. Shape the remaining skin-toned sugarpaste into hands and feet and position onto the figure. You may need short lengths of spaghetti to help hold them in place.

14. Finally, roll out the black sugarpaste into a small circle, cut or indent the edges for hair and arrange on his head.

MAKING THE ACCESSORIES

1. Take 60 g of grey sugarpaste and shape a thin rectangular box for the television.

2. Use the remaining pieces of sugarpaste to make accessories for your figure as shown in the photo. You could have a gaming console and a handpiece, as well as a TV remote, magazines, a pizza box, junk-food wrappers and maybe even a bin brimming over with rubbish!

3. Store the completed cake overnight in a warm, dry place, covered loosely with a tea towel.

LOLLY OVERLOAD

A true crowd-pleaser for kids both young and old, this flying Jet Plane cake is so quick and easy to prepare it is likely to become a firm family favourite.

WHAT YOU'LL NEED

CAKE

23–25 cm round chocolate cake (see Basic recipes, page 12)

1 quantity chocolate buttercream icing (see Basic recipes, page 13)

DECORATIONS

1 kg mixed lollies (including a few Cadbury Jet Planes)

SPECIAL EQUIPMENT

cake decorating wire

ON THE DAY OF THE PARTY

1. Bake the cake and set aside to cool.
2. Make the chocolate buttercream icing and ice the top and sides of the cake.
3. Tip all your lollies – except for a few Jet Planes – into a bowl and mix together.
4. Pick up small handfuls of lollies and press them into the icing, making sure that the top and sides of the cake are totally covered.
5. Cut lengths of cake decorating wire in half and press into the base of the Jet Planes. Poke these into the cake so that they appear to be flying around the top.

NOTE:

- ***Placing candles between the lollies can be tricky, so it is best to just poke them in where you can.***
- ***There are many ways that you can adapt this cake to your own child. You could use your child's favourite lollies, or change the lolly overload to a chocolate overload by covering the cake with chocolate-coated lollies. Place the odd foil-wrapped lolly at random for effect.***

KIWI PARTY CAKE ★★★

This cake is ideal for one-to-three-year-olds, as you can match the number of kiwi and the candles on the little cake with the birthday child's age. Light the candles on the little cake, but bear in mind that they will burn down quickly as they have been trimmed. This cake is best completed the day before the party as it is fairly time-consuming.

WHAT YOU'LL NEED

CAKE

1.5 kg sugarpaste icing
23 cm round cake (see Basic recipes, page 12)
sieved apricot jam, thinned with a little hot water

DECORATIONS

mint green food colouring gel
lemon yellow food colouring gel
brown food colouring gel
Capri blue food colouring gel
golden yellow food colouring gel
7 mini muffins of your choice
candles

SPECIAL EQUIPMENT

2.5 cm plain round cutter
dried spaghetti
pastry brush
plain round icing nozzle

THE DAY BEFORE THE PARTY

Colouring the sugarpaste and making the decorations can be done up to a few days in advance.

1. Colour 700 g of the sugarpaste with the mint green food colouring gel, then add a little lemon yellow food colouring gel to make a good lime colour.

2. Colour 300 g of sugarpaste brown.

3. Colour 200 g of sugarpaste turquoise, by mixing Capri blue and a little lemon yellow.

4. Colour 100 g of sugarpaste golden yellow, for the beaks and feet.

5. You will have 200 g of white sugarpaste remaining. Wrap all the sugarpaste balls in plastic food wrap until ready to use to prevent it drying out.

MAKING THE CAKE

1. Bake the cake and set aside to cool.

MAKING THE KIWI

1. To make the kiwi, take three mini muffins and set aside. These will be the kiwi bodies.

2. Roll a marble-sized piece of brown sugarpaste into a ball for the kiwi heads.

3. Roll out a quarter of the brown sugarpaste to a thickness of 3 mm.

4. Brush a mini muffin with a little of the apricot jam and position a head on top. Cover with the rolled-out brown sugarpaste. Carefully mould it down and over the kiwi's head and body, sealing the ends underneath. Snip off any large amounts of excess sugarpaste with scissors and roll the kiwi around on a flat surface to help smooth it.

5. Repeat step four to make the remaining two kiwi.

6. Mould a small piece of the golden yellow sugarpaste around a 5 cm length of spaghetti to form a beak, leaving 1 cm of spaghetti uncovered to poke into the head (it is a good idea to make a couple of extra beaks in case any get broken). Position the beaks on the kiwi heads.

7. Roll tiny pieces of white icing for the eyes, place above the beak and use a piece of dried spaghetti to press in pupils and help push them in position.

8. Make feet by taking six 4 cm long carrot-shaped pieces of yellow sugarpaste and flattening them a little.

9. Cut three toes and splay them slightly.

10. Bend the feet to form an ankle and poke a short length of spaghetti into the end to help hold them securely to the body. Leave these sitting to harden as you prepare the remaining decorations.

MAKING THE RUG

1. To make the rug, roll out the turquoise sugarpaste to a thickness of 4–5 mm and cut out a 20 cm square. Cut a 10 mm fringe along two opposing ends.

2. Roll out 50 g of lime sugarpaste to a thickness of 4–5 mm.

3. Cut spots out of the turquoise rug with the round cutter and replace them with spots cut from the lime sugarpaste. Set aside a little of this rolled-out lime sugarpaste for the icing on the kiwi cake.

4. Cover the rug with plastic food wrap until you have iced the cake to keep it soft and pliable.

MAKING THE MINI KIWI CAKE

1. Roll out the remaining brown sugarpaste and use this to cover a mini muffin for the little kiwi cake.

2. 'Ice' the cake using a circle of leftover lime sugarpaste.

3. Trim about a third off the bottom of the candles and poke them into the little cake.

4. Roll out the white sugarpaste and cut out a circle for the little cake plate.

5. Place the mini cake on the plate.

MAKING THE PRESENTS

1. Trim the three remaining mini muffins into cubes.

2. To make the present wrapping paper, roll out the white sugarpaste to a thickness of 2–3 mm and cut into three 10 cm squares.

3. Brush the muffin cubes with a little sieved and thinned apricot jam and place one in the centre of each square.

4. Cut the sugarpaste into a cross shape (cutting a square out of the corners) with the muffin in the centre.

5. Fold the sides of the crosses up and press the edges together to seal.

6. Cut tiny circles of yellow, turquoise and lime sugarpaste using the thin end of a plain round icing nozzle. Press onto the presents to make spots. This part can be a little fiddly so you may choose to leave the presents plain.

7. Roll out any sugarpaste offcuts and cut out thin strips. Use these to wrap ribbons around the presents.

ICING THE CAKE

1. Brush the cake with the sieved and thinned apricot jam.

2. On a clean, crumb-free surface very lightly dusted with icing sugar, roll out the remaining 650 g lime sugarpaste to a thickness of 4–5 mm, large enough to cover the cake in one piece.

3. Carefully transfer over the cake, smooth down and trim off any excess.

4. Place the rug on top of the cake. Position the kiwi on the rug and attach their feet.

5. Make the kiwi party hats by rolling the remaining turquoise sugarpaste out to 2–3 mm thick. Cut two 15 mm strips and cut out zigzags along the top edges. Roll these around your finger to form a loop, press the edges together and place on the outer two kiwi heads. Make a small green cone for the centre kiwi's hat.

6. Arrange the mini cake and presents in front of the kiwi.

7. Store the completed cake overnight in a warm, dry place covered loosely with a tea towel.

PIRATE CHEST

This pirate chest, filled entirely with wrapped chocolates, is a chocoholic's delight but you can use any of your little pirate's favourite sweets if you prefer.

WHAT YOU'LL NEED

CAKE

1 quantity cake mixture (see Basic recipes, page 12)

1½ quantities chocolate buttercream icing (see Basic recipes, page 13)

DECORATIONS

sour cola straps

silver cachous

chocolate balls

Cadbury Fudge Duets

Cadbury After Dinner Mints

chocolate coins

SPECIAL EQUIPMENT

20 cm x 16 cm cake tin with high sides

baking paper

stiff cardboard

ON THE DAY OF THE PARTY

1. Bake the cake in the cake tin lined with baking paper.

2. Once the cake is completely cold, cut a 2 cm slice off the top to use as the lid for the chest and hollow out the remaining piece of cake to a depth of 2 cm – leaving a 2 cm rim – to make the chest.

3. Cut the cardboard a little smaller than the cake lid. Later, you will place the cardboard under the cake lid to help support it when it is propped on the chocolates.

4. Arrange the chest on a serving plate. Leave the lid on your work surface – you will ice and decorate it there and put it on the chest at the end.

5. Make the chocolate buttercream icing and carefully ice the top and sides of the lid and the sides and rim of the chest.

6. While the icing is still soft, press the cola straps onto the chest, trimming them to fit, and stud the edges with cachous.

7. Form a string of beads by pressing the chocolate balls onto the icing. Drape them over the edge, down the chest and onto the plate, using a tiny amount of icing to secure the balls to the plate.

8. Fill the chest with the wrapped chocolates, stacking them towards the front, and place the lid on top.

CHOCOLATE
CHOCOLATE
Cadbury

FUNKY HANDBAG

This funky handbag cake is perfect for girls who are interested in fashion, and the use of sugarpaste gives it a slick and realistic look.

WHAT YOU'LL NEED

CAKE

1 kg sugarpaste icing
23 cm round cake (see Basic recipes, page 12)
sieved apricot jam, thinned with a little hot water

DECORATIONS

mint green food colouring gel
lemon yellow food colouring gel
orange food colouring gel
purple food colouring gel
turquoise cachous

SPECIAL EQUIPMENT

30 cm length wire
19 cm plate
ice block stick
3 cm flower cutter

THE DAY BEFORE THE PARTY

You will need to make the handle at least a day before the party to allow it time to harden.

1. Colour 800 g of sugarpaste a vibrant lime green using the mint green food colouring gel with a little lemon yellow for good colour.

2. Colour a small piece of sugarpaste orange for the flower centres, then colour the remaining sugarpaste purple, remembering that the colour will intensify over time (see Colouring sugarpaste, page 10).

3. Take a piece of the lime green sugarpaste and form into a 20 cm x 1 cm sausage.

4. Bend the wire into an even curve to form the bag's handle, checking the size against the tin you will bake the cake in.

5. Press the lime green sugarpaste sausage onto the curved wire and mould it around it so that the wire is completely covered. Leave about 5 cm of wire uncovered at each end so that you can poke these into the cake.

6. Set the handle aside for at least a day in a warm, dry place to harden (see Making sugarpaste decorations and figures, page 11).

7. Wrap all the remaining sugarpaste well in plastic food wrap and set aside.

MAKING THE CAKE

1. Bake the cake. When cool remove from the tin and store overnight in an airtight container or well wrapped in plastic food wrap.

ON THE DAY OF THE PARTY

CUTTING AND ICING THE CAKE

1. Cut the cake in half, brush with the sieved and thinned apricot jam and set aside.

2. Lightly dust your work surface with icing sugar, and roll out half the lime green sugarpaste to a thickness of 4–5 mm, taking care not to get any cake crumbs into the sugarpaste as you need to re-roll the leftovers to make the bag flap.

3. Roll the sugarpaste around a rolling pin and drape over the top and down the sides of one cake half.

4. Carefully fit the sugarpaste down over the cake, smoothing as you go, and tuck it under the cake. Trim off any excess.

5. Repeat with the remaining sugarpaste and cake half.

6. Arrange the cakes standing up, flat sides together, on a serving plate.

7. Roll the remaining lime green sugarpaste into a rough circle 4–5 mm thick. Use a 19 cm plate as a guide and cut a circle for the bag flap.

8. Drape the flap over the top and down one side of the cake.

9. Cut off the shorter side at the join in the top of the cake and press the cut edge in neatly.

10. Use the end of an ice block stick to press stitching around the edges of the flap.

11. Make the clasp by rolling a small piece of lime green sugarpaste into a sausage shape and a marble-sized piece of purple sugarpaste into a ball. Position at the bottom of the flap.

12. Roll out the purple sugarpaste to a thickness of 2–3 mm. Cut flowers using the cutter and position randomly over the cake.

13. Roll tiny balls of orange icing, press onto the centres of the flowers and stud each one with a cachou.

14. Finally, push the handle into the top of the cake.

THE GREAT OUTDOORS ★★

Enjoy a slice of Kiwi heaven with this clean green countryside cake.

WHAT YOU'LL NEED

CAKE

1½ quantities Madeira cake (see Basic recipes, page 12)
3 quantities buttercream icing (see Basic recipes, page 13)

DECORATIONS

mint green food colouring gel
5 ice cream cones
blue jelly crystals
blue party sprinkles
4 Texas-sized muffins of your choice
chocolate-coated raisins or peanuts
green party sprinkles
green Cadbury rainbow buttons
10 green mushroom lollies
7 green lollipops
spearmint leaves
white Pascall marshmallows
white mini marshmallows
black sugar art pen

SPECIAL EQUIPMENT

26 cm x 30 cm sponge-roll tin
baking paper
dried spaghetti

THE DAY BEFORE THE PARTY

MAKING THE CAKE

1. Bake the cake in the sponge-roll tin lined with baking paper that comes well up above the sides of the tin to support the cake as it rises during cooking.

2. Cool and store overnight in an airtight container or well wrapped in plastic food wrap.

ON THE DAY OF THE PARTY

ICING AND DECORATING THE CAKE

1. Place the cake on a large flat serving platter.

2. Make the buttercream icing, and colour half of it a pale green, using the mint green food colouring gel. Remember that the colour will intensify over time. Leave the other half of the icing white.

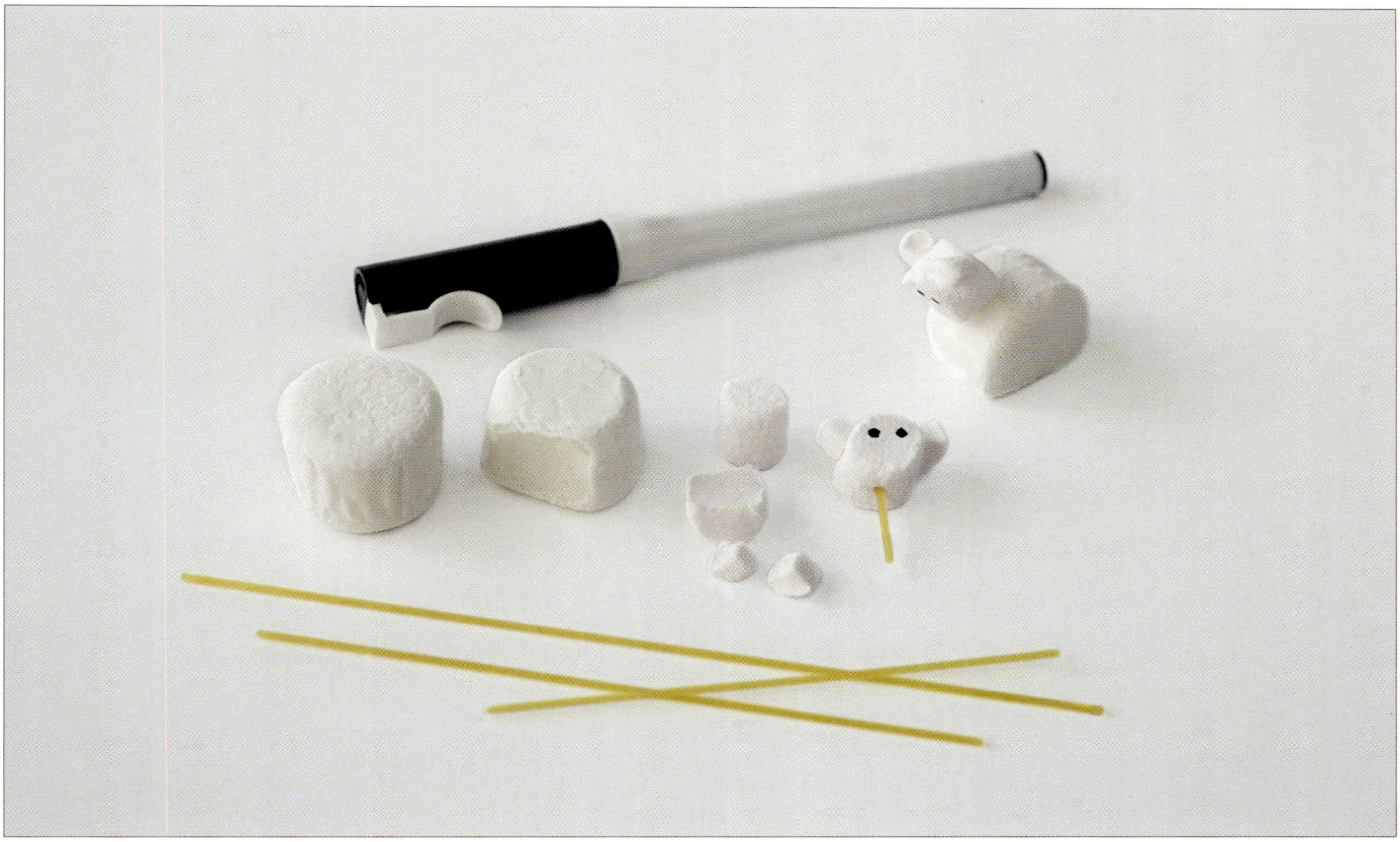

3. Use some of the white buttercream to ice the ice cream cones for the mountains. Sprinkle with a few blue jelly crystals and blue party sprinkles.

4. Position these mountains along the back of the cake.

5. Ice the top and sides of the cake leaving a 'meandering river'-shaped gap running through the icing.

6. Trim the Texas-sized muffins on the bottoms to create rounded hill shapes.

7. Colour the remaining white buttercream a darker green and ice the hills with it. Position these hills in front of the mountains.

8. Fill the riverbed with the blue jelly crystals and a few blue party sprinkles. Make a waterfall by continuing the jelly crystals down the front of the cake and making a pool of them on the plate.

9. Dot chocolate-coated raisins or peanut rocks along the riverbank, and sprinkle green party sprinkles and green rainbow buttons over the hills and plains.

10. Place the green mushroom trees, lollipops and spearmint leaves in groups around the cake.

11. Make sheep bodies by trimming a small slice off the sides of three large white marshmallows.

12. Use mini marshmallows for the heads and cut another mini marshmallow into six pieces to make ears. Press the cut edges of the marshmallow ears to the sheep heads.

13. Use a short length of spaghetti poked into the head to secure it to the body. Draw on eyes using the sugar art ink pen.

14. Finally, position the flock of sheep on your cake.

BUTTERFLY CAKE

★★

This cute little butterfly looks pretty with her lilac body and spotted yellow wings but you can make her any colour you like. If you prefer not to use sugarpaste, make the cake as below but ice with coloured buttercream icing (see note on page 50) and stud the wings with lollies.

WHAT YOU'LL NEED

CAKE

900 g sugarpaste icing
23 cm round cake (see Basic recipes, page 12)
sieved apricot jam, thinned with a little hot water
3 mini muffins of your choice

DECORATIONS

lemon yellow food colouring gel
lilac food colouring gel

SPECIAL EQUIPMENT

baking paper
pastry brush
round cutters
skewer or dried spaghetti
small plain round icing nozzle

THE DAY BEFORE THE PARTY

Colouring the sugarpaste can be done up to a few days in advance.

1. Colour 600 g of sugarpaste with a little lemon yellow food colouring gel.

2. Colour 200 g of sugarpaste with the lilac food colouring gel to make a dark lilac, adding a little at a time and remembering that the colour will intensify over time.

3. Break off about 20 g of this lilac sugarpaste and knead in about 50 g of white sugarpaste to make a pale lilac.

4. Wrap all the coloured sugarpaste in plastic food wrap as you work to prevent it drying out until ready to use.

MAKING THE CAKE

1. Bake the cake and store overnight in an airtight container or well wrapped in plastic food wrap.

ON THE DAY OF THE PARTY

CUTTING AND ICING THE CAKE

1. Cut the cake in half.

2. Trace the butterfly wing template from page 94 onto baking paper and cut out.

3. Place the pattern piece on each half of the cake and cut wings out of the cake using a small serrated knife.

4. Brush the two pieces of cake evenly with the sieved and thinned apricot jam.

5. Halve the yellow sugarpaste and roll out one piece to a thickness of 4 mm.

6. Carefully drape this over one of the wings. Smooth down over the sides and trim off the excess, tucking the edges neatly under the cake. Repeat with the remaining yellow sugarpaste and cake.

7. To make the butterfly's body, remove any paper cases from the mini muffins and brush each with the sieved and thinned apricot jam.

8. Halve the dark lilac sugarpaste and roll out to a thickness of 4–5 mm.

9. Cut three 9 cm circles from the sugarpaste using cutters, and cover the mini muffins completely.

10. Take a small piece of the dark lilac sugarpaste and roll into a 3 cm ball for the tail.

11. Place the butterfly's wings onto a serving plate and position the iced mini muffins in between for the body. Place the tail on the end.

DECORATING THE CAKE

For the butterfly in the photograph we cut out and placed the spots as follows, but you can use any combination or pattern you like.

1. Roll out the remaining dark lilac sugarpaste and cut four 3.5 cm circles and two 2 cm circles.

2. Roll out the pale lilac sugarpaste and cut two 4 cm circles, two 2 cm circles, four 1.5 cm circles and four dots (about 5 mm). The small end of an icing nozzle is ideal for these dots.

3. Arrange the circles and dots on the wings, placing some of the smaller ones on the bigger ones for a nice effect.

4. Roll a thin sausage of dark lilac sugarpaste, shape into antennae and attach above the butterfly's head.

5. Roll two tiny balls of white sugarpaste to make the eyes, then flatten slightly and place on the butterfly's face. Add an even tinier ball of dark lilac for the pupil. Poke the pupil with a skewer or a piece of dried spaghetti to complete the eyes and help fix them to the butterfly head.

6. Shape a smile using a small icing nozzle.

NOTE: If you want to ice the cake using buttercream icing instead of sugarpaste, you will need 1½ quantities of buttercream icing (see Basic recipes, page 13).

LIQUORICE EXPRESS ★★

This train is perfect for liquorice lovers everywhere, but don't feel you have to restrict the cargo to just liquorice. Stack the carriages with any of your favourite lollies or chocolates to delight everyone.

WHAT YOU'LL NEED

CAKE

1 quantity cake mixture (see Basic recipes, page 12)
2 quantities buttercream icing (see Basic recipes, page 13)

DECORATIONS

golden yellow food colouring gel
liquorice logs
60 hundreds-and-thousands-covered liquorice lollies
1 liquorice strap
assorted liquorice allsorts, tubes and twists

SPECIAL EQUIPMENT

seven 6 cm x 9 cm mini loaf pans – or see note on page 53
baking paper

THE DAY BEFORE THE PARTY

MAKING THE CAKES

1. Bake the cakes in the mini loaf pans lined with baking paper. Cool and store overnight in an airtight container or plastic food wrap.

ON THE DAY OF THE PARTY

CUTTING AND ICING THE CAKES

1. Make the buttercream icing and colour it using the yellow food colouring gel. Remember that the colour will intensify over time.

2. Make the engine barrel by rounding off the top of one of the mini loaves. For the cab, prop another loaf up against the end and carve a semicircle out of the back.

3. Use some of the buttercream icing to make a crumb coat (see Using a crumb coat, page 13) and ice the engine so the crumbs don't show through.

4. Once the crumb coat on the engine has dried, carefully ice the carriages (the remaining five mini loaves) and engine with the remaining buttercream icing.

5. Arrange the engine and carriages either on a large plate or tray or have them curving across the table.

DECORATING THE TRAIN

1. Make the wheels by cutting twenty-four 1 cm slices from the liquorice logs. Squash them flat and press a liquorice lolly on top. Place these on the carriages and engine.

2. To decorate the engine, cut a funnel from the liquorice log and position on the engine barrel along with a hundreds-and-thousands-covered liquorice lolly.

3. Flatten a 2 cm slice of liquorice log and press on the front of the engine.

4. Make a cattle catcher out of short lengths of liquorice tubes cut on the diagonal and pressed into the front of the engine.

5. Cut square windows from the liquorice strap and position on the cab of the engine.

6. Cut short lengths of liquorice twists to join the carriages together.

7. Arrange piles of assorted liquorice allsorts, logs and lollies on the carriages.

NOTE: If you don't have mini loaf pans, bake the cake mixture in a 24 cm x 18 cm tin and cut eight rectangles (6 cm x 9 cm) for the engine and carriages. You will have to ice with a crumb coat on the carriages as well as the engine if you make the cake this way.

FLOWERPOT CAKE ★★

This pretty cake makes a charming centrepiece for the table. You may prefer to use the rice bubble mixture from the Volcano cake (see page 18) to fill the pot, instead of baking a cake.

WHAT YOU'LL NEED

CAKE

1 quantity chocolate cake mixture (see Basic recipes, page 12)
1 quantity chocolate buttercream icing (see Basic recipes, page 13)

DECORATIONS

600 g sugarpaste icing
green food colouring gel
pink food colouring gel

SPECIAL EQUIPMENT

5 cm flower cutter
6 cm heart cutter
3 cm circle cutter
2 cm circle cutter
2–3 cm star cutter
toothpick
19 long bamboo skewers
pastry brush
terracotta pot 15 cm high x 18 cm wide
baking paper

THE DAY BEFORE THE PARTY

You will need to make the flowers and leaves at least a day before the party to allow them time to harden.

1. Lightly dust your work surface with icing sugar, and roll out 200 g of sugarpaste to a thickness of 1 cm.

2. Cut eight 5 cm white flowers and lay them on a tray lined with baking paper.

3. Use the green food colouring gel to colour 300 g of sugarpaste.

4. To make the leaves, roll out the green sugarpaste to a thickness of 1 cm and cut out twelve 6 cm hearts. Lay these on the baking paper-lined tray.

5. To make the flower centres, take half the remaining green sugarpaste and knead in a little more green food colouring gel to darken it. Colour another 50 g white sugarpaste a pale pink and 50 g a darker pink.

6. Roll out these four coloured pieces of sugarpaste to about 2–3 mm thickness. Cut out five 3 cm dark pink and three 3 cm dark green circles, and three 2 cm pale pink and three 2 cm pale green circles.

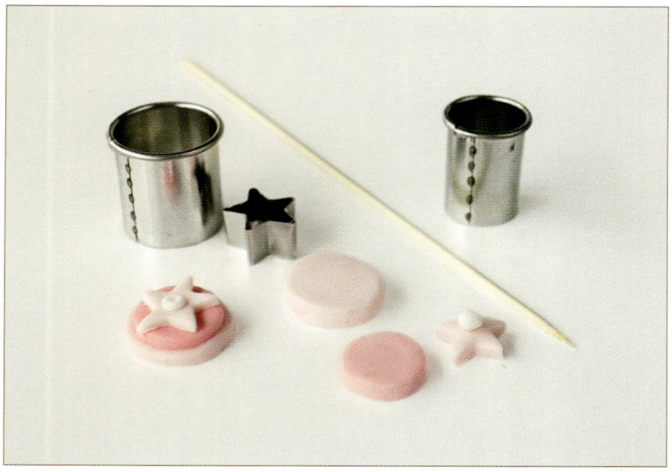

7. Cut out four pale pink stars and two white stars.

8. Lay the smaller circles on the larger circles of the same colour (you will have two dark pink circles left over), and top with a star and then a tiny ball of white icing. Press the white balls on firmly using a toothpick to help them stick and to create a little indentation.

9. Position the six completed flower centres on the white flowers.

10. To make the two swirl flower centres form two pieces of white and pink sugarpaste into 6 cm x 3 cm rectangles.

11. Lay one rectangle on top of the other and roll up into a long sausage shape.

12. Use a sharp knife to cut ½ cm thick slices from the roll. Trim these with a 2 cm round cutter to tidy the edges.

13. Place these swirl circles on the remaining dark pink circles and the last two flowers using a tiny white icing ball and toothpick as before.

14. Use a skewer to make holes in the sides of the flowers and base of the leaves for the coloured skewers to fit into later.

15. Set the flowers and petals aside for at least a day in a warm, dry place to harden (see Making sugarpaste decorations and figures, page 11).

16. Add a little green food colouring gel to water and paint the skewers using a pastry brush. Set aside to dry.

MAKING THE CAKE

1. Wash the pot and line with two layers of baking paper making sure the ends overhang the top so you can lift out the cooked cake later.

2. Make the cake mixture, pour in the lined pot, and bake until a skewer pushed into the middle comes out clean – it will take about 1 hour 20 minutes.

3. When the cake is cool, lift out of the pot. Store overnight in an airtight container or well wrapped in plastic food wrap.

4. Discard the used baking paper as it will be discoloured. Cut two 5 cm wide strips of new baking paper or ribbon and drape them down into the flowerpot so the ends overhang the top. (This will enable you to lift out the cake to serve it later.)

ON THE DAY OF THE PARTY

1. Place the cake back into the pot. Make the chocolate buttercream icing and ice the top of the cake.

2. Press the green skewers into the holes you made on the flowers and leaves and arrange in the cake.

3. To serve, lift the cake out by the strips of baking paper or ribbon.

CREEPY-CRAWLY CATERPILLAR

This bright green caterpillar making its way cheerfully across the table will delight your party guests. You could have one muffin for each child at the party, or have the same number of muffins as the birthday child's age and top each one with a candle.

WHAT YOU'LL NEED

CAKE

1 quantity buttercream icing (see Basic recipes, page 13)
8 un-iced muffins of your choice in paper cases

DECORATIONS

green food colouring gel
lemon yellow food colouring gel
red and green sour worms (you may need 2 packets to get enough of each colour)
2 packets Nestlé Wonka Nerdalicious lollies, or similar
2 small white bracelet lollies, less than 1 cm diameter
1 thin liquorice lace

SPECIAL EQUIPMENT

dried spaghetti

ON THE DAY OF THE PARTY

ICING THE MUFFINS

1. Make the buttercream icing. Colour the buttercream using the green food colouring gel with a touch of the lemon yellow to make a lime green.

2. Ice the muffins generously.

3. To make the spikes, use the back of a teaspoon and press it onto the icing, then gently lift it up to form a peak. Repeat this all over the muffins.

4. Choose the best muffin to use as a head and set aside.

DECORATING THE CATERPILLAR

1. Slice the Nerdalicious lollies into 1 cm pieces and dot them into the iced muffins.

2. Press two small white bracelet lollies firmly into two slices of Nerdalicious lollies for the eyes. Press these onto the muffin head.

3. Cut two short pieces of sour worms for the antennae and press onto the head.

4. Cut a short piece of liquorice lace for the mouth. Press this onto the head and curve to form a smile.

5. Cut about a third off the ends of the sour worms for the legs. Break off short lengths of dried spaghetti and carefully but firmly press into the cut ends.

6. Position a leg on either side of a muffin body, poking the spaghetti in firmly to secure it. You may need to trim the legs a little so that they stand up.

7. Arrange the caterpillar so that it curves across the table or serving plate in an s shape.

***NOTE:** For a completely 'buggy' party try a variation on the Creepy-crawly caterpillar and make individual bug cupcakes (see below) as well.*

HAPPY CAMPER

Kiwi kids love camping – nothing compares to sleeping in a tent under the stars. This little camper is getting ready for a day outdoors with a hearty breakfast.

WHAT YOU'LL NEED

CAKE

1.2 kg sugarpaste icing
2 quantities chocolate cake mixture
(see Basic recipes, page 12)
sieved apricot jam, thinned with hot water

DECORATIONS

skin-toned food colouring gel
golden yellow food colouring gel
brown food colouring gel
black food colouring gel
1 quantity buttercream icing
(see Basic recipes, page 13)
moss green food colouring gel
¾ cup desiccated coconut
Capri blue food colouring gel

SPECIAL EQUIPMENT

large bamboo skewer
small plain round icing nozzle
bottle lid
toothpicks
20 cm square cake tin, at least 12 cm deep
25 cm cake board

THE DAY BEFORE THE PARTY

You will need to make the camper, fire and frying pan at least a day before the party to give them enough time to harden.

COLOURING THE SUGARPASTE

1. Set aside a small ball of white sugarpaste for the fried egg.

2. Colour 50 g of sugarpaste skin tone, 50 g yellow, 50 g brown and 50 g grey using a little black food colouring gel (see Colouring sugarpaste, page 10).

MAKING THE CAMPER

1. Shape the camper's head and neck using two-thirds of the skin-toned sugarpaste.

2. Make his nose by rolling a tiny piece of skin-toned sugarpaste into a ball, shaping one side to a point.

3. Poke a hole in the centre of his face with a toothpick and mould the pointy end of the nose into it.

4. Use the skewer to poke in eyes and the icing nozzle to form a smile.

5. Roll the remaining skin-toned sugarpaste into a sausage shape, cut in half and form into arms.

6. Roll a tiny piece of yellow sugarpaste into a ball for an egg yolk and save a marble-sized piece for the shirt sleeves.

7. Use the remaining yellow sugarpaste to make a rounded rectangular shape for the camper's t-shirt.

8. Secure the arms into the shoulders with a short piece of dry spaghetti and bend the arms in front of his body.

9. Roll the marble-sized piece of yellow sugarpaste into a ball, flatten out and cut in half. Drape this over the top of the shoulders to create shirt sleeves.

10. Use the end of the skewer to make an indentation in the top of the t-shirt for his neck. Poke the head and neck into this hole on top of the camper's shoulders.

11. Take a marble-sized piece of the brown sugarpaste and roll into a 4 cm circle. Use a sharp knife to cut a 1 cm fringe around the edge. Place on top of the camper's head for the hair.

MAKING THE ACCESSORIES

1. Roll the remaining brown sugarpaste into a rough sausage about 30 cm long and 5–8 mm thick. Cut into logs for the camp fire.

2. Roll a 2 cm ball of grey sugarpaste. Use the lid of a bottle and press down on it firmly to shape the inside of the frying pan. Shape the sides of the pan with your fingers.

3. Roll another small piece of grey sugarpaste to make the pan handle and press onto the side of the pan.

4. Make tent poles by moulding a small amount of grey sugarpaste around the top of two toothpicks.

5. Roll the remaining grey sugarpaste into marble-sized rocks to make the camp fire.

6. Form a small circle using the reserved white sugarpaste and flatten for the egg white. Gently press on the yellow egg yolk.

7. Place all these pieces, along with the camper, onto a sheet of baking paper and set aside in a warm, dry place to harden (see Making sugarpaste decorations and figures, page 11).

MAKING THE CAKE

1. Make the cake using the two quantities of cake mixture cooked together in the deep square cake tin lined with baking paper.

2. As it is such a deep cake, it will take longer to cook so allow at least 1 hour 20 minutes. If it starts to darken on top, cover with a sheet of baking paper.

3. Allow to cool for at least 20 minutes before removing from the tin.

ON THE DAY OF THE PARTY

ICING AND ASSEMBLING THE CAKE

1. Make the buttercream icing and colour it moss green.

2. To make the grass, place the coconut in a plastic bag with a little moss green food colouring and mix well.

3. Tip some of the coloured coconut from the bag onto a clean work surface.

4. Use a knife to spread a little buttercream around the side edges of the cake board. Dip each edge into the coconut to cover.

5. Spread the rest of the icing over the top of the board and sprinkle the remaining coconut over it.

6. Find the centre line on top of the cake and cut diagonally out to the bottom edge, on both sides, to make a triangular tent shape from the cake.

7. Colour 700 g of sugarpaste a pale blue, using the Capri blue food colouring gel.

8. Lightly dust your work surface with icing sugar, and roll the blue sugarpaste out to a thickness of 4–5 mm.

9. Use a piece of baking paper to trace a triangular template from the ends of the cake.

10. Using your triangular template, cut three tent ends from the sugarpaste. Re-roll the remaining icing into a large rectangle.

11. Spread the sieved and thinned apricot jam over the entire cake.

12. Press a triangle tent end onto each end of the cake and trim. Drape the large piece of sugarpaste over the top of the cake. Trim to size and press the edges together neatly to seal.

13. Position the tent on the iced board. Place the camper in front of the tent.

14. Cut the remaining blue sugarpaste triangle in half and position around the camper as the tent flap.

15. Arrange the rocks, logs and pan around the camper.

NOTE: If your little camper likes to fish, you could make a fishing rod from a skewer and string (see Fishing kids, page 82) and add a fish to his frying pan.

LOLLY SHOP

★★

This lolly shop cake is sure to be a hit at any party. After all, you can't go wrong with all these lollies! Include a birthday message on the cardboard to personalise the cake.

WHAT YOU'LL NEED

CAKE

1½ quantities chocolate cake mixture (see Basic recipes, page 12)

2 quantities buttercream icing (see Basic recipes, page 13)

DECORATIONS

40 pink fruit sticks

40 orange fruit sticks

50 yellow fruit sticks

a selection of small lollies for the cake

SPECIAL EQUIPMENT

28 cm x 18 cm cake tin with a depth of about 7 cm

baking paper

coloured cardboard

ON THE DAY OF THE PARTY

MAKING AND CUTTING THE CAKE

1. Bake the cake in the deep cake tin lined with baking paper.

2. Once the cake has cooled completely, remove from the tin and place on a large flat serving plate or tray.

3. Cut out a 'step' 9 cm long and 2 cm deep from one end of the cake and move this piece to the back of the cake to form the three tiers of the lolly shop display.

ICING THE CAKE

1. Make the buttercream icing.

2. Cover the cake with a crumb coat (see Using a crumb coat, page 13) and leave to harden before covering it with the final coat.

3. Trim the fruit sticks to size and arrange, alternating the colours, around the sides of the cake.

4. Use the extra yellow fruit sticks to divide up the top of the cake for the lolly display.

5. Position groups of small lollies between the sticks.

6. Cut a square of cardboard, then round off the top into a half circle to fit the back of the cake. Write your birthday message on it, then position at the back of the cake.

NOTE: You will need over 100 fruit sticks to cover the sides. If you think that is excessive, leave the sides plain.

SOCCER SHIRT

This soccer shirt can easily be modified to become a rugby jersey or netball bib (see note overleaf). If you're pressed for time, make the entire cake the day before and store it overnight in plastic food wrap or in an airtight container.

WHAT YOU'LL NEED

CAKE

1 quantity cake mixture (see Basic recipes, page 12)
1 kg sugarpaste icing
sieved apricot jam, thinned with a little hot water

DECORATIONS

blue food colouring gel

SPECIAL EQUIPMENT

38 cm x 26 cm sponge-roll tin
baking paper
ruler
letter cutters

THE DAY BEFORE THE PARTY

MAKING THE CAKE

1. Bake the cake in the sponge-roll tin lined with baking paper. It will only take about 20 minutes to cook so keep an eye on it. Let the cake cool completely before removing it from the tin. Store overnight in a warm, dry place, loosely covered with a tea towel.

COLOURING THE SUGARPASTE

1. Take 900 g of sugarpaste and add enough blue food colouring gel to produce a deep blue. If it becomes too sticky, knead in a little icing sugar. Wrap well in plastic food wrap and store in a warm, dry place overnight.

ON THE DAY OF THE PARTY

CUTTING AND ICING THE CAKE

JACKSON
11

1. Cut a 6 cm strip from one end of the cake and cut this in half. These are your sleeves. Place the cake on a large flat serving plate or tray and position the sleeves.

2. For the V-neck, measure halfway along the top of the cake and make a 6 cm cut down the front. Cut diagonally to 5 cm either side of the original cut to form the V.

3. Brush the entire cake with the sieved and thinned apricot jam.

4. Very lightly dust your work surface with icing sugar and knead then roll out the blue sugarpaste, taking care not to get any icing sugar on top of the sugarpaste. The sugarpaste needs to be large enough to cover the entire cake in one piece.

5. Carefully roll the sugarpaste around a rolling pin and transfer onto the cake. Smooth the icing over the top and sides of the cake and trim off any excess.

6. Roll out the remaining white sugarpaste to a thickness of 3–4 mm.

7. Cut 1.5 cm wide strips, using a ruler as a guide to ensure a straight line. Position these strips on the cake at the hem and neckline and two strips on each sleeve.

8. Use letter cutters to cut out the name of the birthday child from the white sugarpaste.

9. The numbers on the cake need to be around 14 cm high, so either draw them on a piece of baking paper using a ruler or print them off the computer. Cut out your number template and use as a stencil to cut the sugarpaste.

10. Finally, centre the letters and numbers on the shirt.

NOTE:

- ***To make a black rugby jersey, add about a teaspoon of black food colouring gel to 900 g of sugarpaste (wear gloves when working with the gel as it will stain your hands).***

- ***To make a netball bib, make and colour the cake as shown. Roll 300 g of white sugarpaste to a thickness of 2–3 mm, and cut out a bib to fit over the shirt. Decorate with your child's position.***

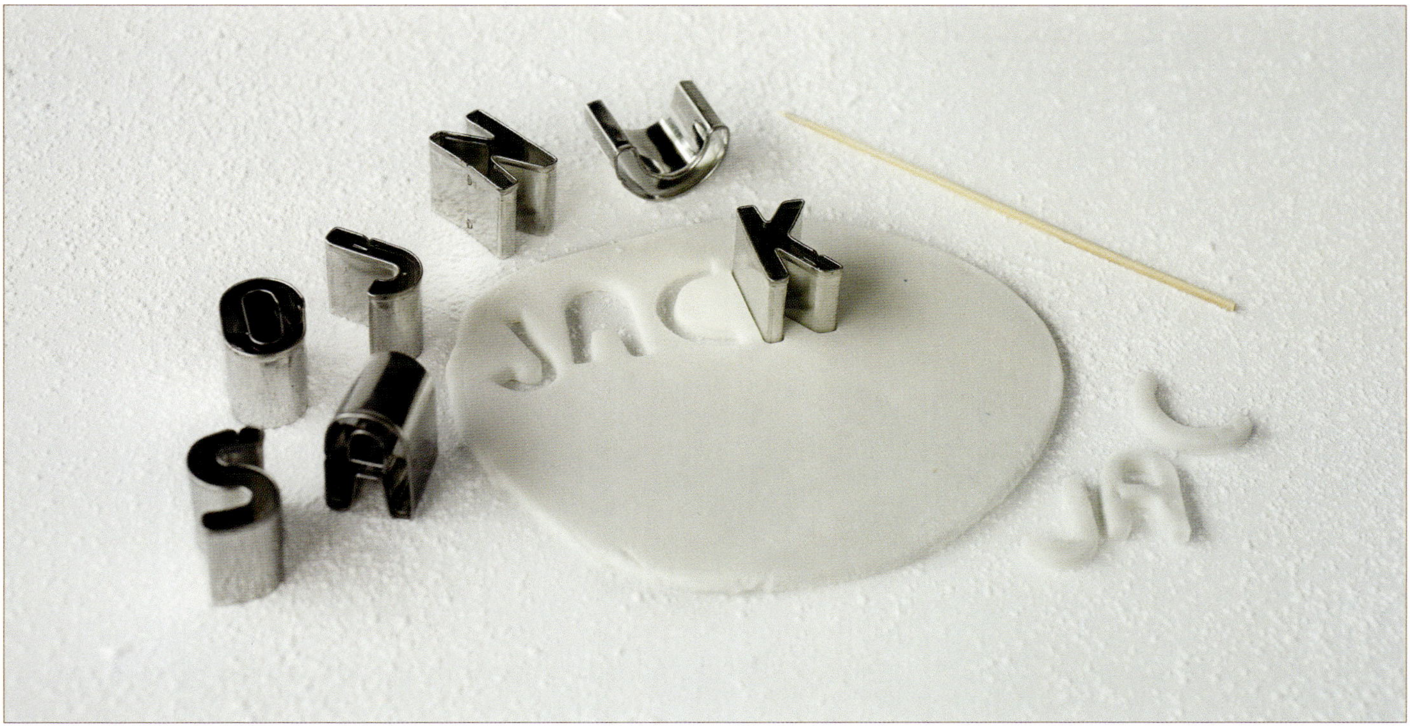

FLOWER FAIRY

WHAT YOU'LL NEED

CAKE

25 cm round cake (see Basic recipes, page 12)
2 quantities buttercream icing (see Basic recipes, page 13)

DECORATIONS

800 g sugarpaste icing
lemon yellow food colouring gel
skin-toned food colouring gel
violet food colouring gel
silver and green cachous
20 purple sugar-coated jubes
20 green sugar-coated jubes
20 lemon sugar-coated jubes
silver edible lustre

SPECIAL EQUIPMENT

4 cm round cutter
7 cm round cutter
corrugated cardboard
thick skewers or wooden spoons
2.5 cm star cutter
5–6 cm flower cutter
2 cm round cutter
toothpick
dried spaghetti
small plain round icing nozzle
garlic crusher

You can either buy a fairy or make your own for this pretty cake, and then base the colour scheme around that of the fairy.

THE DAY BEFORE THE PARTY

The fairy and the petals need to be made at least a day before the party to allow them time to harden.

MAKING THE PETALS

1. Very lightly dust your work surface with icing sugar, and roll out 600 g sugarpaste to a thickness of 3–4 mm.

2. Make the petals by cutting eighteen 7 cm circles and eighteen 4 cm circles.

3. Place the petals onto corrugated cardboard and roll over them lightly using a rolling pin to push the corrugated pattern into them.

4. Pinch one end of the petals together, then lay them on a piece of baking paper. Place thick skewers or wooden spoon handles underneath the rounded petal tips to give them a slight curve.

5. Leave them in a warm, dry place for at least a day to harden (see Making sugarpaste decorations and figures, page 11).

MAKING THE FAIRY

1. Very lightly dust your work surface with icing sugar, and roll out a little sugarpaste to a thickness of 3–4 mm. Cut out a tiny star using the star cutter – this is the fairy's wand. Set this aside on a sheet of baking paper.

2. Take 20 g of sugarpaste and colour it lemon yellow for the hair. Colour 60 g of sugarpaste skin tone for the body and 100 g violet for the dress.

3. To make the dress, roll the violet icing to a thickness of 2–3 mm. Cut out two flowers using the flower cutter. Roll them over the corrugated card to indent the lines, then cut out a 2 cm circle from the middle.

4. Make a pair of shoes using marble-sized pieces of violet icing. Use a thick skewer to poke in a hole for the foot and make a silver buckle using a cachou. Set aside.

5. Use the skin-toned icing to make two 5 cm long arms, scoring a tiny cut for the thumb using a toothpick.

6. To make the legs, mould two 8 cm long skin-toned sugarpaste rolls, slightly carrot shape, and flatten the thicker end slightly for her thighs.

7. To make the fairy's body, roll the remaining violet icing into one 2 cm ball and one 3 cm ball, making the larger ball slightly egg-shaped for the torso.

8. Sit the smaller violet ball on top of the fairy's thighs, then arrange the two flowers overlapping each other to make her skirt. Place the larger violet torso on top.

9. Use the big skewer to poke in shoulder holes for the arms and attach. It may help to use a piece of dried spaghetti to anchor them securely.

10. Poke a piece of dried spaghetti in at the neck and mould a ball of skin-toned sugarpaste around it for the neck.

11. To make the head, roll a large, marble-sized ball of skin-toned sugarpaste.

12. Poke holes for the eyes using a toothpick and use the end of a plain round icing nozzle to shape a smile.

13. To make the hair, roll out a small ball of yellow sugarpaste and push through a garlic crusher. Use a toothpick to remove the strands and position them carefully on the fairy's head.

14. Make the wand using the reserved white star and a piece of spaghetti, and poke it into her hand.

15. Cut wings out of baking paper and attach to the fairy's back with a short length of spaghetti.

16. Drape the fairy's legs over the handle of a wooden spoon so her knees are up, then set aside in a warm, dry place for at least a day to harden (see Making sugarpaste decorations and figures, page 11).

ON THE DAY OF THE PARTY

ICING THE CAKE

1. Make the buttercream icing and colour it using a little of the lemon food colouring gel.

2. Place the cake onto a large flat serving plate, remembering that it will need to be large enough to hold the petals as well.

3. Trim the top of the cake into a dome shape and use a third of the buttercream to make a crumb coat (see Using a crumb coat, page 13).

4. Let the crumb coat harden, then ice again with the remaining buttercream icing.

5. Stipple the icing slightly by repeatedly applying the back of a teaspoon, then lifting it off to raise peaks. Stud with silver and green cachous.

6. Poke the large dried petals in around the base, then arrange the smaller ones on top of these.

7. Press the jubes into the icing around the sides and dust over a little silver edible lustre.

8. Finally, place the fairy on top.

BEACH KIWI

A New Zealand summer usually involves a lot of lazing around at the beach, just like this little kiwi in her bikini. The demerara sugar makes great sand and you can make lots of little accessories out of sugarpaste – be creative and make her accessories relevant to your child.

WHAT YOU'LL NEED

CAKE

23 cm round cake (see Basic recipes, page 12)
1 recipe buttercream icing (see Basic recipes, page 13)
200 g demerara sugar

DECORATIONS

300 g sugarpaste icing
brown food colouring gel
golden yellow food colouring gel
orange food colouring gel
pink food colouring gel
sieved apricot jam, thinned with a little hot water

SPECIAL EQUIPMENT

pastry brush
dry spaghetti
small plain round icing nozzle

THE DAY BEFORE THE PARTY

Colouring the sugarpaste and making the decorations can be done up to a few days in advance.

1. Colour 100 g of the sugarpaste a pale brown for the kiwi, 30 g golden yellow, 50 g orange and 50 g pink.

2. Wrap all the coloured sugarpaste in plastic food wrap as you work to prevent it drying out until ready to use.

MAKING THE TOWEL

1. Form eight pieces of pink sugarpaste into 16 cm long thin rolls. Do the same with the orange sugarpaste, then arrange the lengths alternately to form the towel.

2. Roll out with a rolling pin to flatten and trim the ends. Use a sharp knife to cut a fringe.

3. Transfer the towel onto a baking-paper lined tray and cover with plastic food wrap to prevent it drying out.

MAKING THE KIWI

1. Take about 40 g of the brown sugarpaste and roll it into a muffin-sized ball for the kiwi's body.

2. Roll a marble-sized piece into a ball for the kiwi's head.

3. Roll out the remaining brown sugarpaste to a thickness of 3–4 mm.

4. Place the head and the body together and cover both the head and body with the rolled icing. Tuck the rolled icing underneath and trim off any excess. Smooth all over to form a plump kiwi body.

5. Cut two tiny triangles from the rolled brown sugarpaste to make the wings and press these onto the sides.

6. Take a piece of yellow sugarpaste and mould it around a 5 cm length of dried spaghetti to make a long thin beak, making sure you leave 1 cm of spaghetti showing at the base to secure the beak into the head.

7. Form the remaining yellow sugarpaste into two paddle shapes for the feet. Cut out toes and bend to make an ankle. Use sticks of dried spaghetti to secure to the body.

8. Place the kiwi onto baking paper and attach her feet.

9. Roll out a small strip of pink sugarpaste, cut out the bikini and place on the kiwi. Use the thin end of a small plain icing nozzle to make a pattern on the bikini.

10. Cut sunglasses out of a strip of thinly rolled white sugarpaste, cutting out the lenses using the thin end of a small plain icing nozzle.

11. Place on her face and then poke in her beak.

MAKING THE OTHER ACCESSORIES

1. Roll a 3 cm ball of white sugarpaste for the beach ball.

2. Roll any remaining yellow sugarpaste to a thickness of 2–3 mm and cut out strips for the ball's stripes.

3. Press on the stripes and cover the ends of the stripes with dots of pink sugarpaste. Roll to make a perfect ball.

4. Make a cellphone, book, starfish, shells, or anything else you like using the remaining sugarpaste. Store the kiwi and her accessories on baking paper in a warm, dry place covered loosely with a tea towel.

MAKING THE CAKE

1. Bake the cake and store in an airtight container or well wrapped in plastic food wrap.

ON THE DAY OF THE PARTY

1. Make the buttercream icing.

2. Place the cold cake upside down on a serving plate so that you have a nice flat top to work with (you may need to cut a little off the bottom to level the cake).

3. Ice the top and sides with the buttercream icing.

4. Gently sprinkle over the demerara sugar and press onto the top and sides of the cake to make the sand.

5. Finally, arrange the sugarpaste decorations on the cake.

BIRTHDAY BURGER

★★★

The ever-popular, classic New Zealand takeaway looks almost like the real thing in this burger and chips cake. It will have universal appeal and is suitable for both children and adults alike.

WHAT YOU'LL NEED

CAKE

1.5 kg sugarpaste icing
23 cm round cake (see Basic recipes, page 12)
sieved apricot jam, thinned with a little hot water

DECORATIONS

red food colouring gel
pink food colouring gel
brown food colouring gel
yellow food colouring gel
green food colouring gel
2 un-iced Texas-sized muffins of your choice
1 tablespoon sesame seeds

SPECIAL EQUIPMENT

pastry brush
letter cutters
toothpicks

THE DAY BEFORE THE PARTY

Colouring the sugarpaste and making the decorations can be done up to a few days in advance.

1. Colour 800 g of the sugarpaste bright red (see Colouring sugarpaste, page 10). Don't be concerned if you can't get it quite vivid enough, as the colour will develop.

2. Break off 25 g of the red sugarpaste and work some pink food colouring gel into it to make a beetroot colour.

3. For the burger fillings, colour 50 g of sugarpaste dark brown, 25 g yellow and 25 g green.

4. Colour 300 g a very pale brown, adding a touch of yellow to make a 'bread' colour for the bun and chips.

5. Wrap all the coloured sugarpaste in plastic food wrap as you work to prevent it drying out until ready to use.

MAKING THE CAKE

1. Bake the cake and store overnight in an airtight container or well wrapped in plastic food wrap.

MAKING THE BURGER AND CHIPS

1. Cut the tops off the Texas-sized muffins and brush these with the sieved and thinned apricot jam.

HAPPY BIRTHDAY

2. Roll the pale brown sugarpaste to a thickness of 3–4 mm and cover the two muffin tops completely. Make sure you don't get any crumbs in the icing.

3. Pour a small pile of sesame seeds onto a plate and press the top of one of the two muffins firmly into them so that the seeds stick. This will be the top bun of the burger.

4. Re-roll the remaining pale brown sugarpaste to a thickness of 1.5 cm and cut into 1.5 cm thick strips. Cut these into varying lengths to make the chips.

5. Roll out the green sugarpaste into a 6–7cm circle and crinkle the edges to make the lettuce leaf.

6. Roll out the beetroot-coloured sugarpaste and cut a 6 cm circle to make the beetroot.

7. Mould the dark brown sugarpaste into a 6 cm meat patty and poke little holes around the edge using a toothpick.

8. Roll out the yellow sugarpaste to a thickness of 3–4 mm and cut a 6 cm square to make the cheese.

9. Assemble the burger and cover it and the chips loosely with a tea towel. Store overnight in a warm, dry place.

ON THE DAY OF THE PARTY

ICING THE CAKE

1. Place the cold cake on a serving plate and trim the top flat if it is too rounded.

2. Brush with the sieved and thinned apricot jam.

3. Dust a work surface very lightly with icing sugar, then roll out the red sugarpaste icing to a thickness of about 5 mm, and big enough to cover the cake in one piece.

4. Roll the sugarpaste loosely around a rolling pin and transfer onto the cake.

5. Smooth down and trim off any excess.

6. Roll out the white sugarpaste to a thickness of 3–4 mm and use the letter cutters to cut out the words HAPPY BIRTHDAY. You might also want to cut out your child's name to add.

7. Press the letters carefully around the side of the cake.

8. Knead the leftover white sugarpaste together and roll out to a thickness of 3–4 mm.

9. Cut into a 20 cm square and place it on top of the cake, draping to resemble a hamburger wrapper.

10. Finally, place the burger on the white sugarpaste paper on the cake and pile the chips around it.

SUMMER JANDALS

The classic Kiwi footwear makes a fabulous and simple-to-make summer cake.

WHAT YOU'LL NEED

CAKE

1 quantity cake mixture (see Basic recipes, page 12)
1½ quantities buttercream icing (see Basic recipes, page 13)

DECORATIONS

pink food colouring gel
green lolly straps
small round pastel lollies
2 fish lollies or other lolly of your choice

SPECIAL EQUIPMENT

25 cm x 35 cm sponge-roll tin
baking paper
cake decorating wire

ON THE DAY OF THE PARTY

1. Bake the cake in the sponge-roll tin lined with baking paper that extends well above the tin's sides to catch any overflow. Set aside to cool.

2. On baking paper, trace around the template on page 95 and cut out. Place this pattern on the right-hand side of the cake and cut around it with a sharp knife to make one right-foot jandal cake. To create a left-foot jandal, flip the pattern over. Position it on the cake and cut around it as before.

3. Place the jandal cakes on a large flat plate or serving platter, dusting away any crumbs.

4. Make the buttercream icing and use a tiny amount of pink food colouring gel to tint it pale pink.

5. Use about a third of the icing to do a crumb coat (see Using a crumb coat, page 13). Set aside to harden. Once the crumb coat has dried, ice the cakes with the remaining icing. If you need to soften the buttercream, heat it for a few seconds in the microwave.

6. Cut the cake decorating wire in half and poke into the cake where indicated on the template to form the supports for the jandal straps. Position the green straps over the supporting wires, and press the remaining green straps around the edges of the cake.

7. Finally, press the pastel lollies onto the buttercream to make spots and position the fish lollies between the straps.

FISHING KIDS

★★★

WHAT YOU'LL NEED

CAKE

1.2 kg sugarpaste icing
1 quantity chocolate cake mixture (see Basic recipes, page 12)
sieved apricot jam, thinned with hot water
½ quantity buttercream icing (see Basic recipes, page 13)

DECORATIONS

black food colouring gel
brown food colouring gel
skin-toned food colouring gel
blue food colouring gel
orange food colouring gel
green food colouring gel
black sugar art pen

SPECIAL EQUIPMENT

1.5 litre bowl
baking paper
dried spaghetti
2 bamboo skewers
toothpick
small plain round icing nozzle
garlic crusher
cotton sewing thread
small star cutter
table knife or small artist's palette knife

New Zealand kids love to spend a day outside, and what could be more enjoyable than fishing by the sea? This is a relatively time-consuming cake to make and ice so it is a good idea to complete most of it the day before, leaving only the waves to make on the day of the party.

THE DAY BEFORE THE PARTY

Colouring the sugarpaste can be done up to a few days in advance.

1. Take 700 g of the sugarpaste and add a little black food colouring gel and a tiny amount of brown food colouring gel to make a grey-brown colour, remembering that the colour will intensify over time (see Colouring sugarpaste, page 10).

2. Knead until the colours are almost completely worked in but the icing still retains a slightly marbled look.

3. Take the remaining 500 g white sugarpaste and colour 80 g skin tone, 80 g blue, 50 g black, 50 g orange and 50 g green. Leave the remaining sugarpaste white.

4. Wrap all the sugarpaste in plastic food wrap until ready to use to prevent it drying out.

MAKING, CUTTING AND ICING THE CAKE

1. Bake the cake in the 1.5 litre bowl lined with baking paper.

2. Once the cake is cool, carve a crescent-shaped rock out of the cake creating a ledge for the children to sit on. Place on a flat serving plate or cake board.

3. Use some of the offcuts to make smaller rocks and position these around the sides.

4. Brush away all crumbs and lightly cover the whole cake with the sieved and thinned apricot jam.

5. Lightly dust your work surface with icing sugar and roll out the grey-brown sugarpaste to a thickness of 4–5 mm.

6. Roll loosely around a rolling pin and carefully lay it over the cake. Mould it around the rocks.

7. Trim the edges and use these icing offcuts to shape smaller rocks to dot around the base.

MAKING THE FIGURES

It is best to make and place the figures on the cake straight away to ensure that they sit well.

1. To make the legs, roll half the blue icing into a 12 cm long sausage. Trim the ends – these will form the bottoms of the jeans.

2. Fold the jeans in half and position on the cake so that they are 'sitting' on the rock ledge. If you are making the figures in advance, shape into a sitting position.

3. Shape a pair of gumboots out of the black sugarpaste and use a piece of spaghetti to secure these to the base of each leg of the jeans.

4. Make a t-shirt body and two carrot-shaped upper arms using the green sugarpaste. Using a skewer, poke holes into the body where the head and upper arms will go, then position the arms in place (see Making sugarpaste decorations and figures, page 11).

5. Use the skin-toned sugarpaste to make the forearms and hands, and attach these to the green upper arms using spaghetti poked through the centre to hold them securely in place.

6. Roll a head out of the skin-toned sugarpaste and poke a large hole in the base with a skewer.

7. Poke holes for the eyes using a toothpick and use the end of a plain round icing nozzle to shape a smile.

8. Roll a tiny ball of skin-toned sugarpaste to make the nose and press onto the face.

9. Form a neck out of skin-toned sugarpaste and press one end into the head. Position the other end of the neck into the hole previously made in the t-shirt.

10. To make the hair, roll out a small ball of black icing and push through a garlic crusher. Use a toothpick to carefully position these strands on top of the figure's head.

11. Cut a bamboo skewer in half and tie a length of cotton thread around the end to make the fishing line.

12. Position the skewer into the figure's hands so that they are holding the fishing rod.

13. Repeat this process to make the second figure, but this time use white sugarpaste for the t-shirt.

MAKING THE ACCESSORIES

1. Add a little white sugarpaste to the remaining skin-toned sugarpaste and make a flax kete. Use a knife to score a woven pattern on the front.

2. Make a chilly bin using some of the orange sugarpaste, with a white lid and handle.

3. To make the seagulls' bodies, form small pieces of skittle-shaped white sugarpaste, then attach small flat wings on the sides.

4. Make tiny carrot-shaped beaks using orange sugarpaste and attach to the seagulls' heads.

5. Use the sugar art pen to draw the seagulls' feathers and eyes.

6. Poke a short length of spaghetti into the bottom of the seagulls and use this to secure them to the rocks.

7. Use any remaining orange sugarpaste to make fish and starfish (with a small star cutter), and attach these to the rocks. Use a dab of water to secure if needed.

8. Use the sugar art pen to draw dots on the rocks for limpets and mussels.

9. Store the cake overnight in a warm, dry place loosely covered with a tea towel.

ON THE DAY OF THE PARTY

MAKING THE WAVES

1. Make the buttercream icing. Set aside a small amount of white for the whitecaps and colour the remainder blue.

2. Spread the blue buttercream over the cake board or plate, using a table knife or small artist's palette knife to sculpt waves. It is a good idea to practise on a separate plate first to hone your technique.

3. Top the waves with a little of the white buttercream to make whitecaps.

4. Finally, press the ends of the figures' fishing lines into the waves.

SKATEBOARDER

If you like, your party guests can 'tag' this cake themselves using sugar art pens. You can either buy a skateboarder figure or make one using sugarpaste.

WHAT YOU'LL NEED

CAKE

800 g sugarpaste icing
2 quantities cake mixture (see Basic recipes, page 12)
sieved apricot jam, thinned with a little hot water

DECORATIONS

80 g sugarpaste icing (if making the skateboarder figure yourself)
blue food colouring gel
lime green food colouring gel
skin-toned food colouring gel
black food colouring gel
brown food colouring gel

SPECIAL EQUIPMENT

toothpick
dried spaghetti
small plain round icing nozzle
20 cm x 20 cm square cake tin with deep sides
baking paper
pastry brush
black sugar art pen

THE DAY BEFORE THE PARTY

The skateboarder will need to be made at least one day before the party to allow time to harden.

MAKING THE SKATEBOARDER

1. If you are making the skateboarder, colour 20 g of sugarpaste pale blue and 20 g of sugarpaste lime green. Colour three small pieces of sugarpaste the following colours: skin tone, dark grey and brown.

2. Colour the 800 g of sugarpaste for the cake at the same time. Colour this a pale grey using the black food colouring gel, remembering that the colour will intensify over time (see Colouring sugarpaste, page 10). Wrap all the pieces well in plastic food wrap and set aside.

3. Roll out the lime green sugarpaste and cut out a tiny number for the t-shirt, then form the remainder into a skateboard deck about 5 cm long.

4. Roll the dark grey sugarpaste into four tiny balls for the wheels. Flatten them slightly, poke a toothpick into the centre and draw each wheel centre with the sugar art pen.

5. Use a small ball of the pale grey (from the 800 g for the cake) and knead in a little of the blue icing to make the blue for his trousers. Shape into a fat triangle and cut to form the legs. Use the toothpick to add stitching detail.

Happy Birthday
ELLIOTT
ALICE
Jack
Bella

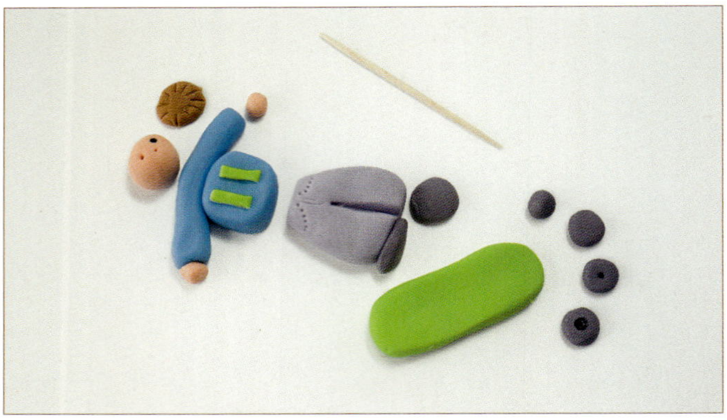

6. Make two flat feet out of the dark grey icing.

7. Use the skin-toned sugarpaste to form a head and two hands. Use the toothpick to poke in eyes and the icing nozzle to form a smile.

8. Finally, roll a tiny piece of brown sugarpaste into a flat circle and cut the hair. Place on the figure's head.

9. Piece the figure together, beginning with his feet on the skateboard and working upwards. Leave the wheels off the skateboard at this stage. Skewer a stick of dried spaghetti through the body to hold it together and set aside in a warm, dry place to harden.

MAKING THE CAKE

1. Bake the cake and store overnight in an airtight container or well-wrapped in plastic food wrap.

ON THE DAY OF THE PARTY

CUTTING AND ICING THE CAKE

1. Cut the cake in half diagonally. Place the two triangular top sides together to make the ramp. Place on a flat serving plate or tray.

2. Using a bread knife, carve out a concave curve to make the quarter pipe.

3. Trim off the top of the ramp and use these offcuts (or pieces of sugarpaste) to plug any gaps between the cakes.

4. Sweep away the crumbs and brush the cake with the sieved and thinned apricot jam.

5. Very lightly dust your work surface with icing sugar and roll the pale grey sugarpaste out to a thickness of 5 mm. You need to be able to cover the cake completely using one piece of sugarpaste, so measure up and over the highest part of the cake to ensure your sugarpaste is wide enough to cover it.

6. Roll the sugarpaste loosely around a rolling pin, brushing off any icing sugar from the back as you do so, and drape over the cake.

7. Carefully mould it down and around the cake. You will need to trim pieces from the sides. Use scissors, as these will help seal the edges by pressing them together as you cut. Trim the sugarpaste around the base of the cake and tuck under neatly.

8. Use a black sugar art pen or black food colouring gel painted on with a small paintbrush to 'tag' the cake.

9. Place a small blob of icing under the skateboard to raise it off the cake enough for you to be able to place the wheels alongside. Position the skateboarder on the quarter pipe.

NOTE: The amount of icing needed to cover this cake may seem excessive, but it does need to be rolled quite thickly to be able to cover the cake in one piece.

KIWIANA CHRISTMAS

Built around a polystyrene cone and decorated with classic New Zealand lollies, this makes a wonderful Christmas Day centrepiece. With 40 mini muffins, there will be plenty for everyone.

WHAT YOU'LL NEED

CAKE

600 g sugarpaste icing
1 quantity buttercream icing (see Basic recipes, page 13)
40 mini muffins of your choice in paper baking cases

DECORATIONS

green edible art gel
black sugar art pen
Cadbury Jaffas
spearmint leaves
green cachous

SPECIAL EQUIPMENT

bamboo skewer
2.5 cm star cutter
4 cm star cutter
6 cm star cutter
25 cm tall polystyrene cone with base diameter of 10 cm, available at craft and sewing stores
toothpicks or cocktail skewers

THE DAY BEFORE THE PARTY

The sugarpaste kiwifruit and stars can be made up to a week in advance.

MAKING THE KIWIFRUIT SLICES

1. To make the kiwifruit slices, colour 170 g of sugarpaste green.

2. On a work surface lightly dusted with icing sugar, roll the green sugarpaste out to a rectangle measuring 30 cm x 5 cm.

3. Roll 30 g of white sugarpaste into a 30 cm long roll and lay down the centre of the green rectangle.

4. Wrap the green around the white and press the edges together to seal.

5. Roll the kiwifruit tube on a flat surface to smooth it off. Try not to stretch it too much.

6. Cut off 1 cm slices and flatten them out to a thickness of 1–2 mm. Cut with small circle cutters 3–4 cm in diameter to get even circular shapes.

7. Lay the kiwifruit slices on a sheet of baking paper and use a bamboo skewer to press in a 'spoke' pattern radiating out from the white centre.

8. Using the edible ink pen, draw dots for seeds around the white centres. Set aside in a warm, dry place to harden (see Making sugarpaste decorations and figures, page 11).

MAKING THE STARS

1. To make the stars, roll 400 g of the white sugarpaste to a thickness of 1 cm and cut out as many stars of both sizes as you can from the icing. Cut one 6 cm star for the top. Set aside with the kiwifruit slices to harden. Wrap the small amount of remaining sugarpaste well in plastic food wrap to prevent it drying out until ready to use.

ON THE DAY OF THE PARTY

1. Make the buttercream icing and ice the mini muffins.

2. Attach each iced muffin to the polystyrene cone using toothpicks, working from around the base upwards and placing them snugly together.

3. Decorate the tree by pressing kiwifruit slices on top of some of the muffins and Jaffas on others. Fill in the smaller gaps with spearmint leaves.

4. Attach the stars to the cone by placing a blob of the reserved soft sugarpaste to the back of each star. Push a toothpick into the soft icing and poke the other end into the cone between the muffins. Place the 6 cm star on the top muffin.

5. Finally, stud the entire tree with green cachous. Merry Christmas!

PACIFICA MERMAID, PAGE 24

BUTTERFLY CAKE, PAGE 48

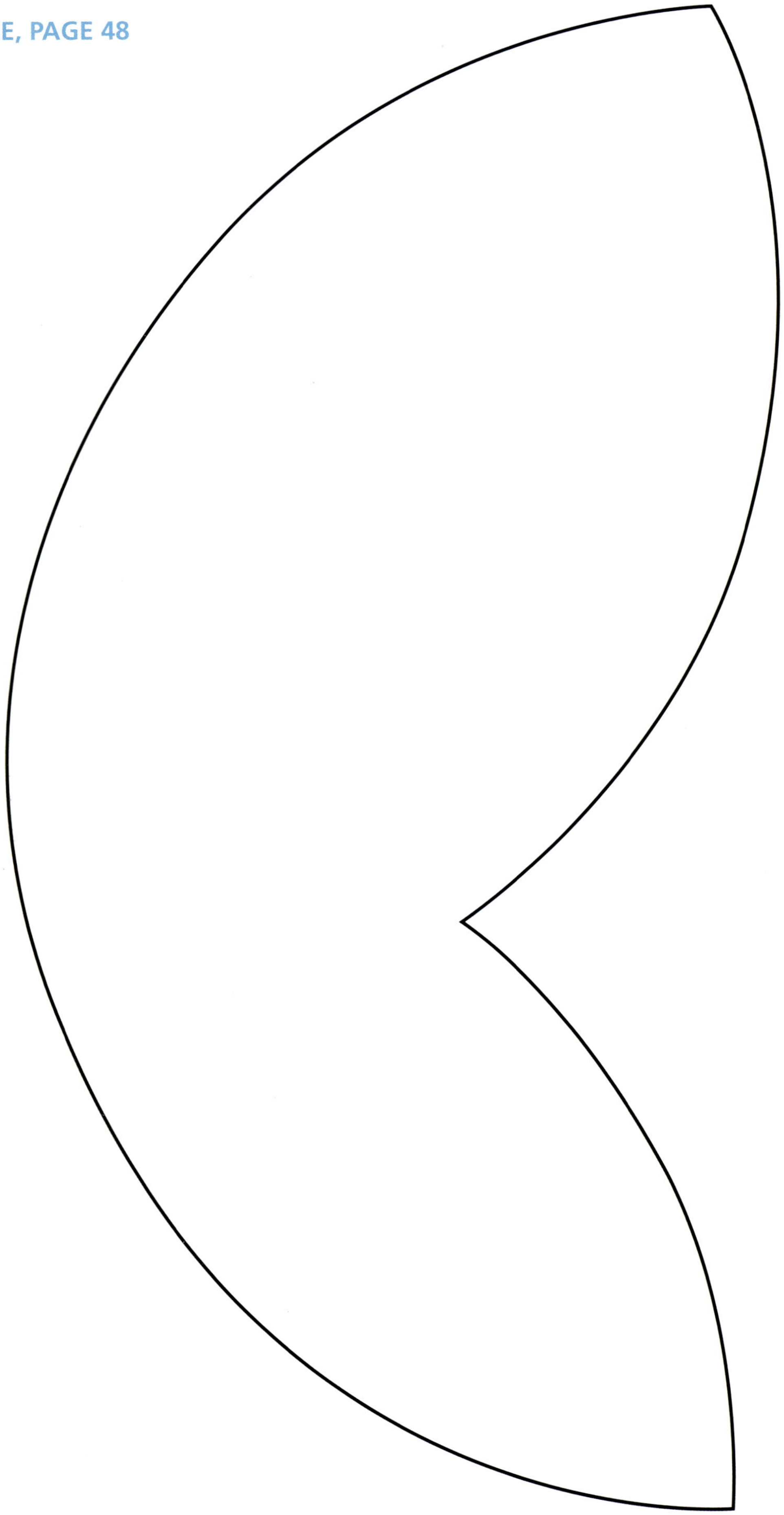

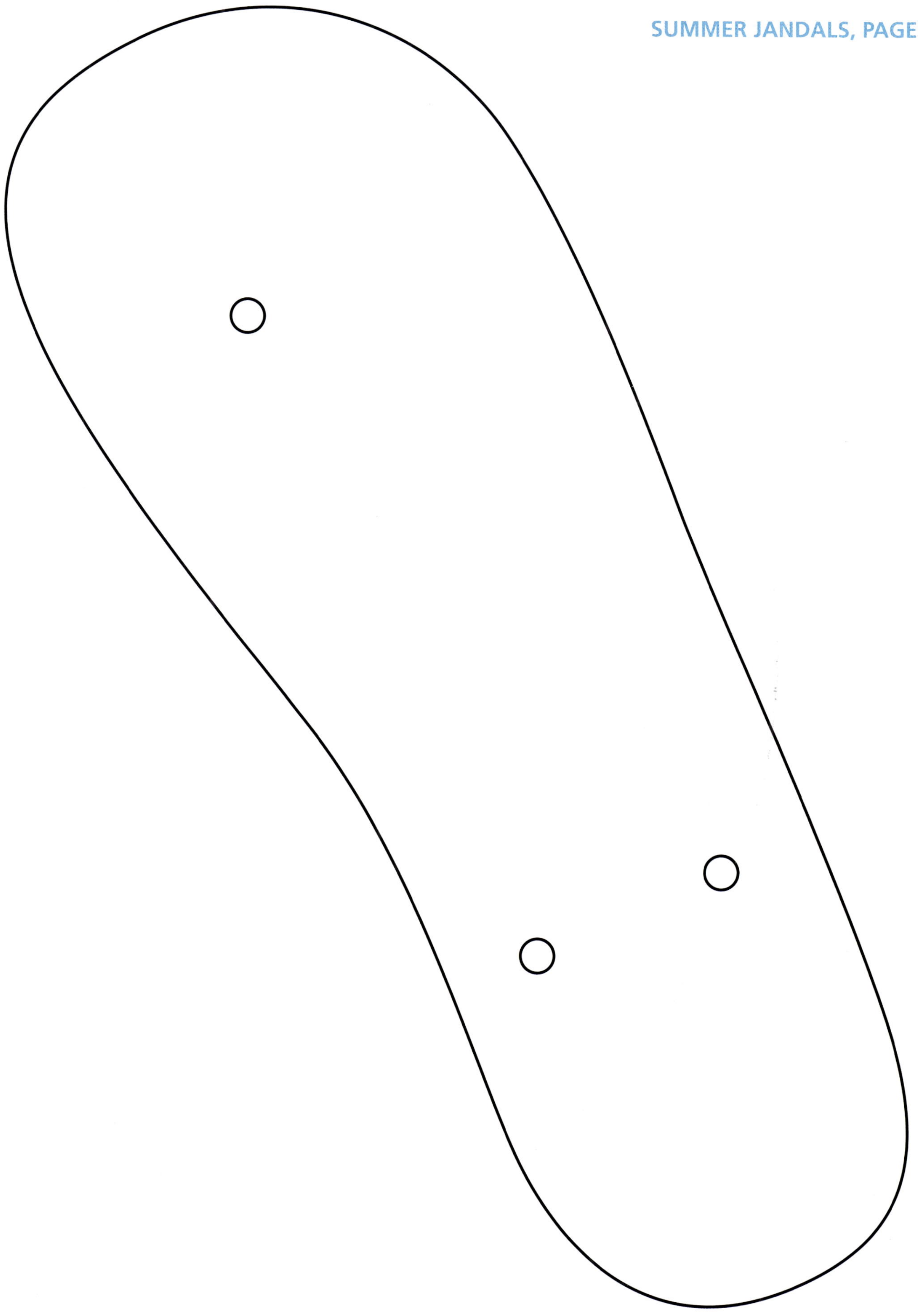

INDEX

Italicised entries indicate cake projects. Numbers in **bold** indicate cake photos.

ACKNOWLEDGMENTS

We would like to extend a huge thank you to Nicola whose experience and patience led a couple of rookies through the photography process and made all our cakes look so great. We had a fabulous time. To Louise Armstrong and Georgina McWhirter at New Holland, thank you for your guidance, support and patience with our project. To John, Elliott, Fraser and Gabrielle Hislop, thank you for allowing us to turn your house upside down on photography days and for eating way more cake and lollies than was necessary. To Greg, Jack and Alice Alexander, thank you for putting up with Linda's long absences and for your unfailing love and support … and for eating cake. Thanks to Kevin Marshall from Bakels in Tauranga for providing wonderful products. Thank you to Zenda and Matt Johns for your support on photo shoot days, and many thanks to Sherryl Jordon for your advice.

Annette and Linda